D0560833

Duns Scotus Library
LOURDES
UNIVERSITY
6832 Convent Blvd.
Sylvania, OH 43560

231.15
M18

L

22

MIRACLES

MIRACLES

A CATHOLIC VIEW

Dr. Ralph M. McInerny

Our Sunday Visitor Publishing Division
Our Sunday Visitor, Inc.
Huntington, Indiana 46750

Copyright © 1986 by Our Sunday Visitor Publishing Division,
Our Sunday Visitor, Inc.
ALL RIGHTS RESERVED

With the exception of short excerpts for critical reviews, no part of this book may be reproduced in any manner whatsoever without permission in writing from the publisher. Write:
Our Sunday Visitor Publishing Division
Our Sunday Visitor, Inc.
200 Noll Plaza
Huntington, Indiana 46750

International Standard Book Number: 0-87973-540-6
Library of Congress Catalog Card Number: 86-61141

Cover design by James E. McIlrath; photo by John A. Zierten

PRINTED IN THE UNITED STATES OF AMERICA

540

Acknowledgments

Scripture texts contained in this work are taken from the *Revised Standard Version Bible, Catholic Edition,* © 1965 and 1966 by the Division of Christian Education of the National Council of the Churches of Christ in the U.S.A., and used by permission of the copyright owner. Special thanks go to the Costello Publishing Co., Inc., for the use of brief excerpts taken from *Vatican Council II: The Conciliar and Post-Conciliar Documents,* © 1975 by Costello Publishing Co., Inc., and Rev. Austin Flannery, O.P., general editor. Other sources from which material has been excerpted or has served as the basis for portions of this work are cited throughout this volume. If any copyrighted materials have been inadvertently used in this book without proper credit being given, please notify Our Sunday Visitor in writing so that future printings of this work may be corrected accordingly.

For
Chauncey Stillman

Contents

Introduction

We Catholics believe that God exists, that he willed the universe to come into being from nothing, and that it would return to nothingness were he to withdraw his sustaining causality. Some two thousand years ago, God the Father sent God the Son to reconcile sinful man with his Creator. God the Son, through Mary and the power of God the Holy Spirit, came into this world as a human being, who was named Jesus. Jesus lived obscurely in an obscure part of the world until he was thirty, when he began a whirlwind of preaching and wonder-working until he was put to death by the occupation government, the Romans, at the instigation of some of the leaders of his own people, the Jews. Three days after his execution, he appeared to his followers, alive and well. He met with them on and off for forty days and then ascended into heaven, promising to return. In the meantime, his followers — the Church — continue to announce the good news. At the end of time, every human person will be raised from the dead, the sheep will be separated from the goats, and so it will be forever and ever.

It is well, from time to time, to realize what an extraordinary thing our faith is. The above summary deliberately states it in the somewhat skeptical tones of that elusive creature, modern man. And modern man, confronted with this summary, is likely to say, "Anyone who will believe that, will believe anything." That Christians also believe in miracles seems scarcely to add a new element. The whole thing is a pack of miracles.

Before asking whether belief in miracles is a separable aspect of Christian faith or merely a summary description of it, we can concede only half the point. The whole point would have it that Christians have been rendered so credulous by their essential beliefs that they are unable to draw the line *anywhere*. But of course we, as individuals and as a Church, *do* accept some marvels as miracles and reject others, if for no other reason than that the belief — in principle, that miracles can and do occur — does not commit us in advance to accept everything that is put forward as a miracle. There are, as we shall see, many reasons for hesitation.

It was Chesterton who said that the man who loses his faith does not then believe in nothing; he is far more likely to believe in anything. This turns the skeptic's charge back upon himself, or at least upon the faithless multitudes. Who has not been struck by the veritable deluge of astrological books, newspaper columns, and radio and television programs, of the past few years? In what prides itself as being the Scientific Age there has been a remarkable increase in superstition. Furthermore, from Robert Ripley to Leonard Nimoy, there are those who put before the public one wonder after another. Claims by people to have been visited by aliens from other planets, even of being taken captive and flown away in a spaceship, are regularly featured. Plenty there to marvel at, certainly.

Is it the Christian who is disposed to accept such accounts as true? Surely not. Not even when suggestions are made that Jesus himself came from another planet and then returned to it. For the believing Christian, Jesus is Almighty God become man, not a visitor from outer space. Nonetheless, the Christian is well advised to realize that his own beliefs, including the belief that miracles occur, strike some nonbelievers as of a piece with stories of the Siberian who lived over two hundred years, of flyings saucers, of reports of psychic phenomena. It would be a rare Christian indeed who would want to make common cause with these others in the hope that a united front by all who hold odd beliefs will prove a problem for the skeptic.

One Characteristic of Miracles

A first note of the miraculous emerges from such considerations. It is not as tales of the strange and wonderful alone that miracles address themselves to our faith. Miracles are not meant to amuse or divert or to frighten or titillate. No marvelous occurrence that does not draw our attention to the central mysteries of Christianity, to the saving work of Jesus Christ, is going to be thought of as a miracle. The miracle will always be a sign of God's presence and an opportunity for men to respond to the divine call. This essential mark of the miracle is almost by itself sufficient to distinguish miracles from mere wonders, whether of the county fair sideshow variety or more complicated ones. It may be hard to find a single positive characteristic of the latter. Sometimes they amuse; often they disgust or frighten.

Astrology will seem a different matter, because it is. The assumption of astrology is that the stars exercise a predictable influence over human affairs and that it is possible to become adept at reading them and thereby to know what is going to happen. Two aspects, then: the influence of the stars, and a species of determinism. If we only knew, we would know that tomorrow is already decided. And the stars give us the means of knowing. That is the attraction of astrology. It is a way of taking the mystery out of the future. This is an old dream and one that was intertwined with the beginnings of modern science. Indeed, in some of its current manifestations, astrology assumes many of the mannerisms of science. Astrology as well as fortune-telling, the reading of tea leaves, and other similar beliefs falls under the general category of superstition, which is condemned by the Church.

Fideism

One of the greatest dangers to the faith today is what the Church calls fideism. Fideism is the view that nothing that we know with unaided reason counts either for or against what we believe. Faith obeys radically different laws than reason, and the believer should not, indeed cannot, relate what he believes to what men (including nonbelievers) can know about the world.

The appeal of fideism in recent times is perhaps due to an assault upon the faith by many philosophers and scientists which lasted for over a century. These critics demanded that the claims of Christianity be subjected to the same standards as any other claims. The implication of course was that Christianity was bound to fail the test. Indeed, the implication was that if one had to invent a set of claims in order to illustrate what could not meet the demands of reason, one could scarcely do better than Christianity.

Believers responded to this attack in several ways, without noticeable effect on their adversaries and with some adverse effects on themselves. That assault has slackened, now that the self-appointed champions of reason have been unable to give a consistent account of the "demands of reason" that does not render their position self-destructive. What a relief it is for believers suddenly to learn that it is at least as philosophically respectable to hold religious beliefs as any other. The faith is describable as a self-contained language game that need not be translatable into some other language game taken to contain the basic criteria of reasonable belief. The attraction is all the greater because faith *is* in many ways unique. The mysteries of faith *cannot* be described or proven on purely natural grounds. Nonetheless, fideism is a great error.

It is also a very large topic to which I cannot here give the attention it deserves. I mention it, nonetheless, to underscore the fact that, if miracles must always relate to the central mysteries of our faith, *these central mysteries are truths, and it is the highest use of the human mind in this life to accept them as such.* Our faith bears on the Ultimate Truth: God. Miracles always relate to the faith. That is why a belief in miracles is not a vacation from reason, a little holiday from the tedious demands of rational responsibility. Not only is it reasonable to believe that miracles can and do happen, it is unreasonable to think they cannot and do not occur.

On Being Reasonable

It is well to remember Cardinal Newman's observation that it is unreasonable to demand that "reasonable" always mean the same thing. No more should we imagine that there is some single method to be followed if acceptable reasonable behavior is to be had. The notion that it is the "scientific method" and it alone that assures the correct use of our reason may be called scientism. It is not of course to be equated with science. It is a belief about what the successes of science commit us to with regard to the use of our minds generally.

Scientism typically has a more sanguine view of the achievements of science than scientists do. We shall not for the moment concern ourselves with that, but rather assume the most unequivocally positive results of scientific inquiry. Nor will we demur at the suggestion that there is an easily describable and recognizable procedure answering to the phrase "the scientific method." The assumption of scientism is that with the successes of science we at last have a method of universal applicability which will enable us to test any and every claim to see if it is rationally acceptable.

One of the famous rejections of Christianity — or any other religious belief — relied on the claim that it is immoral to give one's assent to a proposition on insufficient evidence. The objection invokes the notion of science as a procedure whereby we gather evidence, thanks to which it becomes morally okay to accept certain statements as true. The great difficulty with the assumption is that sooner or later someone is bound to ask if the claim itself has been subjected to the recommended procedure.

It was the downfall of logical positivism in our own day that, having put forward what it called the principle of verifiability — a universal test for any remark that professed to be about the things that are — it was helpless to say where the principle had come from, since it was neither about the things that are nor a logical truth like "A = A." The much vaunted demand for a no-nonsense application of the principle of verifiability as the only rational guarantee of our empirical beliefs employed a principle which could not itself be rationally guaranteed.

The dream of a univocal, simple, and universal method is an old one. Few nowadays would regard it as more than a dream. It has become increasingly difficult to ignore that the way we use our minds in deciding what to do is quite different from the way we use our minds in doing geometry. If there is a "problem of knowledge" it consists of relating such different uses of reason, not in eliminating all but one as impostors. That the diverse uses of our mind vary because they bear on quite different kinds of object seems clear. But it by no means follows from this that these uses of our mind are in all ways different.

Someone who recommended a use of our mind that regularly violated the principle of contradiction would rightly meet with opposition. For all that, "reasonable" is a term with many, even if related, meanings. It is what St. Thomas Aquinas calls an analogous term. And the gift of faith is, for Thomas, a virtue of intellect, one which perfects intellect in its grasp of truth. Thus faith will be compared with science and opinion and other mental activities without, however, being reduced to them. The comparison exhibits likenesses and unlikenesses. It is the possibility of the comparison which underlies the rejection of fideism. It is the diversity that underlies the rejection of scientism.

The Modern Mind

The modern mind to which I alluded at the outset may be characterized as one impressed by the successes of the sciences, however little the possessor of that mind may himself understand science. We are used to the assertion or implication that the modern mind can no longer accept the claims of Christianity. This suggests a near equation of the modern mind and the acceptance of scientism. That nonbelievers should suggest that modern man cannot accept the faith because it is thought to collide with science is not surprising. It *is* surprising to find that many believers assume the same thing about the modern mind and go on to make the modern mind regulative of talk about the faith.

It is as though one were required to make the faith attractive and acceptable to people who by definition adopt the view that the claims of faith *cannot* be true. Our surprise would diminish if what were meant is that such a thing as the modern mind exists, alas, and we believers must relieve people of its burden so that a serious obstacle to faith may be removed. But some seemingly wish Christianity to be reexpressed in such a way that it meets the demands of those for whom it is by definition incredible. This has led to surprising consequences in the work of some theologians.

There are those who think that one of the happy results of the ecumenical council Vatican II is that it put miracles on a back burner, so to speak. Much is often made of the fact that nowadays what is called a "moral miracle" can substitute for miracles in the usual sense in the canonization process. The implication is that the Church is letting it be understood, without saying so explicitly, that the magisterium is as skeptical of miracles in the old sense as is the modern mind.

I am not calling into question moral miracles nor casting aspersions on their use in the canonization process. I am merely suggesting that there is a way of welcoming moral miracles which sees them as so-called miracles, there not being any other kind.

Given the hope of addressing the modern mind involved in the policy mentioned above, it is not surprising to find the same kind of debunking going on in the case of the mysteries of faith.

The Scriptures

The miracles attributed to Jesus in the Gospels — curing the sick, raising the dead, feeding a large crowd with a few loaves and fishes — are treated by some theologians as an embarrassment. If such theologians view miracles in this manner, imagine what the modern mind would say about these biblical events!

What the modern mind would say is that our Lord's miracles did not happen because they could not have happened. "I agree," a certain type of theologian replies. Is he thereby rejecting the Gospels and the long tradition of Christian belief in these matters? Often he will say not. Rather, he suggests that we must interpret such scriptural accounts in a special way. The special way comes down to reading them as if they do not mean what they say. The motive for so torturing a text is, again, the assumption that what they say happened could not have happened, so the texts cannot really say what they say.

This is a path which, once embarked upon, seems to tilt forward, making progress along it ever swifter. Some version of this method has been applied to those scriptural passages in which Christ reveals that he is both human and divine, in which he founds the Church, in which he predicts his resurrection and, more importantly, is said to have risen from the dead. The interpreter goes at such texts under the apparent assumption that we somehow know none of these things actually happened.

Oddly enough, it is precisely at this point that fideism in its most rampant contemporary form may show itself.

Demythologizing and Fideism

The real historical accounts in the Scriptures, before they were overlaid with the notions of later generations, show us, we are told, a Jesus who was just a man among men who did not think of himself as different from you and me. This historical Jesus made a big impression on people, but he didn't work any miracles and he did not found a church. Rise from the dead? What this means is that his followers, in an effort to express their sense that the work of Jesus went on with them, began to talk about his rising from the dead. And so on. The scriptural texts which have traditionally been thought to ground such articles of the creed as the resurrection can no longer be taken to do so.

Are we then to stop believing that Jesus is God and man, that he worked miracles, and all the rest? Apparently not. Believers accept these things, but they should not think they have any scriptural warrant for them. Indeed, Scripture, properly understood, *says the exact opposite, expresses the contradictory, of what we believe.* But to suggest that in these circumstances one could go on believing is to make a mockery of both faith and reason. The believer would be someone who believes that A is true but who knows — thanks to Scripture scholarship — that $-A$ is true, and who still thinks it is all right for him to go on believing that A is true. That is fideism with a vengeance.

I have mentioned these matters in order to underscore the relation between Christian belief as such and belief in miracles. To think and talk about miracles is not to concern ourselves with a peripheral and unimportant matter.

What is a miracle? Thus far, the one feature of the miracle that I have insisted on is that it is a wonderful occurrence essentially linked to the truths of faith. The purpose of miracles is to direct the mind to the good news of Jesus: in that it differs from all kinds of other marvels and wonders, real and natural, as well as from the performances of magicians.

St. Bernadette

As I was working on this book, I made a pilgrimage to the town of Nevers, which is a few hours by train from Paris. There, in the convent of St.-Gildard, Bernadette Soubirous became a nun and it was there that she died. So what? Bernadette was the girl to whom the Blessed Virgin Mary appeared at Lourdes more than a century ago. But it was not those apparitions as such that brought me to Nevers. What enticed me was the fact that the miraculously preserved body of Bernadette is there — in a glass casket, so that one can view it. Although she died in 1879, her body has not corrupted, thereby giving the viewer the impression that, lying there, rolled slightly to one side, she is alive, merely sleeping.

Does that catch your interest? More than likely, but you might think it is just one of those amazing oddities. However rare, the case of the body of St. Bernadette is not unique. As it happens, there are many bodies of saints which have been preserved from corruption. Not by embalming, not by mummification as with Lenin and the pharaohs, but without human intervention at all. Why? The marvel of these incorrupt bodies calls our attention to what the saint did when alive. St. Bernadette's body is a reminder of what she was told during the apparitions of Mary.

Do not think that people beat a path to Nevers simply to look at Bernadette's body. Certainly there are some who, out of a morbid curiosity, do come for that reason;

but the majority are there because they believe in the miraculous. The day I was there, there were perhaps two dozen people at a noon Mass on a weekday in February, most of them from the town.

Lately, just about everybody has heard of the Shroud of Turin, but how many know the origin of the picture of Our Lady of Guadalupe on the cape of the Indian to whom she appeared? When I was young, many knew of Theresa Neumann, a stigmatist who reportedly never ate. The wounds on her body were a vivid reminder of Christ's passion and death. St. Francis of Assisi also bore the wounds of Christ on his body. And, as you probably know, Padre Pio — who died in 1968 — was one of the best-known stigmatists of our time.

If one were to collect information on all such marvels that one way or another bear witness to the truth of Christianity, a very large book indeed would be the result. This work is not that book, even though we mean to discuss the question of miracles with reference to real claimants to the title.

What Lies Ahead

This introduction has thrown before you a great many things. In the chapters that follow I shall attempt to give as accurate and faithful — and believing — an account of the Catholic view on miracles as I can. The book, like Caesar's Gaul, is divided into three parts.

First, we will look at the way Holy Scripture treats of miracles, first in the Old Testament, then in the New with the miracles of Jesus, and conclude with those wrought by the disciples after Jesus' resurrection.

Second, we will take a look at the role miracles have played in the devotion of the faithful over the centuries, with particular though not exclusive reference to the Middle Ages. One of the great phenomena of the medieval period was the pilgrimage to the tomb of St. James the Apostle at Compostela in Spain. We have a thirteenth-century guidebook for the pilgrimage. The Dominican convent of St.-Jacques in Paris, where St. Thomas Aquinas lived and taught, as well as the Rue St.-Jacques, is named from this pilgrimage. You may be more familiar with Chaucer's account of a pilgrimage to Canterbury to visit the tomb of St. Thomas à Becket. There is a traditional link between pilgrimages and miracles, and it seems right to include here present-day pilgrimages. We have all seen the ads in diocesan papers and other publications for Father Felicity's guided tour of the Holy Land, or, more often, of Fátima or Lourdes. The living continuity of Catholic spiritual life through the ages is visible here. There is always a liturgical dimension to such pilgrimages.

In the third part, we will look at what is somewhat grandly called the theology of miracles. Learned believers down the ages, in commenting on Scripture, or in independent studies, have discussed the nature of miracles. The doctrine, as is so often the case in theological matters, culminates in the teaching of St. Thomas Aquinas, but we must take note as well of subsequent and current theological reflection. We will also look at what the official teaching magisterium has to say on miracles. Both theory and practice are important here. We will notice what priests and bishops do when a miracle is alleged to have happened or when someone claims that our Lord or the Blessed Virgin Mary appeared to him. The official caution shown on such occasions should not be taken as skepticism, nor should an ultimate sanction be considered pious credulity. What we have here is a vivid example of the Church reading the signs of the times. In living memory, two popes have visited Fátima, in Portugal, where the Blessed Virgin appeared to three peasant children in 1917, one of whom is still alive at this writing. It would be odd indeed if the ordinary Catholic did not reflect on those visits and draw appropriate conclusions for his own spiritual life. In concluding, we will go back to the extraordinary happenings mentioned above. There has been a veritable explosion of the miraculous in this age of the modern mind.

Miracles are meant, first of all, to get our attention. This little book has a similar aim, though I hope it won't be considered "a miracle" if it attains it. Belief in miracles will already play some role in the life of any Catholic. I think it is important that our response to the miraculous grow and deepen according to the mind and heart of the Church. Miracles are not diversionary occurrences, a simple appeal to wonder, or an MTV interval in the life of the Church.

Miracles are meant to bring us closer to our Creator

and Lord, for whom nothing is impossible. Finally we are all like the doubting St. Thomas. We want a sign. We want to put our hands in the wounds. This is a profound human need, and miracles are thus another instance of the way God's plan for our salvation takes into account the needs of our nature.

DR. RALPH M. MCINERNY
University of Notre Dame

PART ONE

Miracles
in Scripture

Prologue

God reveals himself to man through the created world because the things that are made give us an intimation of their divine cause. But God revealed himself in a special way to our first parents, Adam and Eve, and thereafter to his chosen people through the prophets. All the promises God made are fulfilled in Jesus. The Fathers of Vatican II, in the "Dogmatic Constitution on Divine Revelation" (*Vatican Council II: The Conciliar and Post-Conciliar Documents*), tell us, "The Christian economy, therefore, since it is the new and definitive covenant, will never pass away; and no new public revelation is to be expected before the glorious manifestation of our Lord Jesus Christ. . ." (No. 4).

The Apostles and their successors, by their preaching and ministry, continue to present to men God as revealed in Jesus Christ. "Thus, the apostolic preaching, which is expressed in a special way in the inspired books, was to be preserved in a continuous line of succession until the end of time" (No. 8). This apostolic teaching develops in the Church under the inspiration of the Holy Spirit. "Sacred Tradition and sacred Scripture, then, are bound closely together, and communicate one with the other. For both of them, flowing out from the same divine wellspring, come together in some fashion to form one thing, and move towards the same goal. Sacred Scripture is the speech of God as it is put down in writing under the breath of the Holy Spirit" (No. 9). The task of preaching and preserving this word of God faithfully, explaining it, disseminating it, falls to the successors of the Apostles. The maxim *sola scriptura* does not capture the Catholic outlook, since it is from both tradition and Scripture that the Church draws its certainty about everything that has been revealed.

The Church is the custodian, guarantor, and interpreter of Scripture. "Sacred Tradition and sacred Scripture make up a single sacred deposit of the Word of God, which is entrusted to the Church. By adhering to it the entire holy people, united to its pastors, remain always faithful to the teaching of the apostles, to the brotherhood, to the breaking of bread and the prayers. . ." (No. 10).

This is an important reminder, not only for this part of our little book, but for the whole. If we look first to Scriptures for light on the notion of miracles, then to the practices of the faithful over the centuries, and finally to Church teaching, we do not consider these to be independent and autonomous sources of Catholic doctrine on miracles. "It is clear, therefore, that, in the supremely wise arrangement of God, sacred Tradition, sacred Scripture and the Magisterium of the Church, are so connected and associated that one of them cannot stand without the others. Working together, each in its own way under the action of the one Holy Spirit, they all contribute effectively to the salvation of souls" (No. 10).

The Catholic Church holds that the books of both the Old and New Testaments in their entirety and in all their parts have been written under the inspiration of the Holy Spirit. That is, they have God as their author and that is how they are handed on by the Church. All the books of the Bible teach firmly, faithfully, and without error the truth God wanted put into writing for the sake of our salvation (see No. 11). St. Paul said it: "All scripture is inspired by God and profitable for teaching, for reproof, for correction, and for training in righteousness, that the man of God may be complete, equipped for every good work" (2 Timothy 3:16-17).

Scripture must be read with an eye to the nature of its parts, their literary form, since the truth is proposed and expressed differently in a historical book than in prophecy, poetry, or other types of speech. The reader must take into account the circumstances in which a part of the Bible was written and the way in which customs of the times influenced the mode of expression. Continuing to quote the "Dogmatic Constitution on Divine Revelation," such attention should not, however, fragment the Bible: ". . . no less attention must be devoted to the content and unity of the whole of Scripture, taking into account the Tradition of the entire Church and the analogy of faith, if we are to derive their true meaning from the sacred texts" (No. 12). The Bible is a whole, the parts of which comment on one another, contributing to the overall purpose of written revelation. And we must also be guided by the living tradition of the Church, the use and interpretation of Scripture which is a part of tradition. The parallel between Scripture and Christ unites the aspects of revelation. "Indeed the words of God, expressed in the words of men, are in every way like human language, just as the Word of the eternal Father, when he took on himself the flesh of human weakness, became like men" (No. 13).

Our search in Scripture for light on miracles falls into three parts:

√ Miracles in the Old Testament.

√ The Miracles of Jesus.

√ Miracles of the Apostles.

CHAPTER ONE

Miracles in the Old Testament

The books of the Old Testament have echoed down the ages, inspiring the artist, the poet, the theologian, and indeed the novelist. In our own literature, thanks in large part to the Protestant tradition, biblical themes and rhetoric are prominent, from *Moby Dick* to *East of Eden*. Even now, with secularism all but triumphant, it is common for the Bible to be taught "as literature." There has been a proliferation of translations of the Bible, but the Douay and King James versions continue to retain their hold on the mind and imagination of many.

When Vatican II mentions the need to take into account the literary forms of the different books of the Bible, we should not understand this as an invitation to read the Bible "as literature." One wishes that the biblical commentaries and animadversions of the great French Catholic poet Paul Claudel were available in English. Claudel held that, as a poet, he could respond to the literary forms of the Bible, but he never confused it with any merely human literature. Indeed, Claudel was opposed to the founding of the Biblical School in Jerusalem and carried on a minor feud with Père Lagrange. Perhaps he would have said that the real threat to seeing the Bible for what it is comes not from treating it "as literature" but rather from certain types of biblical criticism.

We need not go into such matters here. Our guide will be the "Dogmatic Constitution on Divine Revelation" of Vatican II, from which we quoted amply in the prologue to this part. With particular reference to the miracles recounted in the Old Testament, we shall see its books as having their chief purpose to prepare both for the coming of Christ — the universal Redeemer — and the messianic kingdom. This is announced by prophecy and shown by various types. "God, the inspirer and author of the books of both Testaments, in his wisdom has so brought it about that the New should be hidden in the Old and the Old should be made manifest in the New" (No. 16).

In the Old Testament, God's power is made manifest in signs and wonders. "Then Moses answered, 'But behold, they will not believe me or listen to my voice, for they will say, "The LORD did not appear to you." ' The LORD said to him, 'What is that in your hand?' He said, 'A rod.' And he said, 'Cast it on the ground.' So he cast it on the ground, and it became a serpent; and Moses fled from it. But the LORD said to Moses, 'Put out your hand, and take it by the tail' — so he put out his hand and caught it, and it became a rod in his hand — 'that they may believe that the LORD, the God of their fathers, the God of Abraham, the God of Isaac, and the God of Jacob, has appeared to you' '' (Exodus 4:1-5).

Later on, in the same book, God says to Moses, " 'Behold, I make a covenant. Before all your people I will do marvels, such as have not been wrought in all the earth or in any nation; and all the people among whom you are shall see the work of the LORD; for it is a terrible thing that I will do with you' '' (34:10).

The miracles of Moses alone would require an extended narrative: the striking of the rock to bring forth water, the dividing of the Red Sea, manna in the desert. Such wonderful deeds are what they are and, at the time and in the context, show forth the power of God and serve to underwrite the authority of his human spokesman. But they also suggest prefigurings of Christ. Jesus himself, when he is asked by the hostile for a sign, says that the only sign that will be given to so wicked a generation is the sign of Jonah. Thus the wonderful survival of Jonah in the belly of the whale for three days prefigures the three days in the tomb before Christ's resurrection. The manna in the desert is taken to prefigure the Eucharist. In the decapitation of Holofernes by Judith, we can find a figure of the Blessed Virgin Mary.

The learned discuss the Old Testament accounts of

wonderful deeds in terms of the Hebrew words employed to designate them. Did the Israelites have the concept of a miracle (as we will develop it in Part 3 of this book)? The notion of literary form is often invoked to suggest that such narratives are a species of tall story that should not be taken literally. Perhaps what we need now is a warning against a skeptical reading of such accounts. We must not let considerations of literary form mask an unwillingness to admit that miracles could and did occur in biblical times. The power of God was made manifest to his chosen people and such manifestations play an important role in the preparation for the new dispensation. God become man in Jesus Christ establishes his authority by signs and wonders.

CHAPTER TWO

The Miracles of Jesus

"When the wine failed, the mother of Jesus said to him, 'They have no wine.' And Jesus said to her, 'O woman, what have you to do with me? My hour has not yet come.' His mother said to the servants, 'Do whatever he tells you.' "

Thus does Chapter 2 of John's Gospel begin the account of the first miracle Jesus wrought, at the marriage feast of Cana. That he acted at the request of his mother is worth noting. It is as if his hour, which had not come, comes because she asks. The story itself is more than familiar. Jesus instructs the servants that the jars used for purification should be filled with water. When the chief steward tastes the water-become-wine he pronounces it better than what has hitherto been served.

John ends the account by saying, "This, the first of his signs, Jesus did at Cana in Galilee, and manifested his glory; and his disciples believed in him" (2:11).

The changing of the water into wine is called a sign. Through it Jesus manifests his glory and as a result his disciples believe in him. The servants who filled the jars with water and drew forth wine for the steward to taste also knew what had happened, but the account does not suggest that the attention of the bride and groom and all the other guests was drawn to what had happened. Nonetheless, with this deed Jesus emerges from the obscurity of the first three decades of his life and sets out on his public ministry. The disciples whom he had already chosen seem to be the primary targets of this extraordinary deed. They witnessed what had happened and believed in Jesus.

The Gospels recount for us both the things Jesus said and the things he did, and among the things he did are a great number of miracles. But the Gospel miracles do not begin with things Jesus did. There is the great miracle of the Virgin birth in which Mary gives birth to a baby both human and divine who has no earthly father. We may want to include among these wonders the dreams of St. Joseph and the star the Magi saw. But the miracles wrought by Jesus himself begin, according to St. John the Evangelist, with the marriage feast at Cana.

Here is St. Matthew's account concerning the beginning of the public ministry of our Lord: "And he went about all Galilee, teaching in their synagogues and preaching the gospel of the kingdom and healing every disease and every infirmity among the people. So his fame spread throughout all Syria, and they brought him all the sick, those afflicted with various diseases and pains, demoniacs, epileptics, and paralytics, and he healed them. And great crowds followed him. . ." (4:23-24). The teaching and the wonder-working go together, the miracles lending authority to what Jesus says.

There is a tradition which divides the miracles performed by Jesus into four major kinds: (1) those which involve spiritual substances, as in the casting out of demons; (2) those involving heavenly bodies; (3) those involving humans; and (4) those involving lesser creatures.

Casting Out Devils

"And immediately there was in their synagogue a man with an unclean spirit; and he cried out, saying, 'What have you to do with us, Jesus of Nazareth? Have you come to destroy us? I know who you are, the Holy One of God.' But Jesus rebuked him, saying, 'Be silent, and come out of him!' And the unclean spirit, convulsing him and crying with a loud voice, came out of him" (Mark 1:23-26). The people are amazed, wondering by what authority Jesus can command even unclean spirits to obey him. But the answer is given by the unclean spirit itself. The demon acknowledges Jesus as "the Holy One of God."

The casting out, or expulsion of, demons in the country of the Gerasenes across from Galilee is even more dramatic. When our Lord "stepped out on land, there met him a man from the city who had demons; for a long time he had worn no clothes, and he lived not in a house but among the tombs. When he saw Jesus, he cried out and fell down before him, and said with a loud voice, 'What have you to do with me, Jesus, Son of the Most High God? I beseech you, do not torment me.' For he had commanded the unclean spirit to come out of the man. (For many a time it had seized him; he was kept under guard, and bound with chains and fetters, but he broke the bonds and was driven by the demon into the desert.) Jesus then asked him, 'What is your name?' And he said, 'Legion'; for many demons had entered him. And they begged him not to command them to depart into the abyss. Now a large herd of swine was feeding there on the hillside; and they begged him to let them enter these. So he gave them leave. Then the demons came out of the man and entered the swine, and the herd rushed down the steep bank and into the lake and were drowned" (Luke 8:27-33).

What is noteworthy about these miracles is that the unclean spirits acknowledge who Jesus is. We find in this the point of Jesus' miracles: that who he is and what his mission is might be manifest. When Jesus casts out an evil spirit that is dumb (Luke 11:14) there is no such acknowledgment and the scribes charge that Jesus is himself possessed and that he casts out devils with diabolic power. In his reply to this, Jesus says that a house divided against itself cannot stand. The devil cast out devils? Would they say this of all who have previously done this? The scribes will be judged by those predecessors of Jesus who have also exorcised unclean spirits. "But if it is by the finger of God that I cast out devils, then the kingdom of God has come upon you" (Luke 11:20). So here, it is Jesus himself who points to the significance of the miracle he performs.

Controlling Heavenly Bodies

"It was now about the sixth hour, and there was darkness over the whole land until the ninth hour, while the sun's light failed. . ." (Luke 23:44-45). St. Thomas Aquinas follows Dionysius in seeing this darkness as the result of a lunar eclipse which, occurring when it did, involves not one miracle but four. For a lunar eclipse to take place at the time of the Jewish Passover means it occurred when sun and moon were in opposition rather than in conjunction. This was not the time when a lunar eclipse would naturally take place.

The second miracle is that about the sixth hour the moon was seen together with the sun in the middle of the sky but in the evening appeared in its proper location, in the east, opposite the sun.

The third miracle consists of the fact that the eclipse proceeded from the east toward the west, rather than from the west toward the east as would normally be the case.

Finally, it was not natural that the moon should proceed from the west to eclipse the sun and then return to the west.

Aquinas notes that St. John Chrysostom sees a fifth miracle in the fact that while a natural eclipse is soon over, this one lasted three hours.

The star of Bethlehem, contrary to what was suggested above, is numbered among the miracles of Christ by Aquinas and he notices that Christ's power over heavenly bodies is shown when he is at his weakest, namely, when he is an infant and when he is nailed to the cross.

Miracles of the kind under discussion were fittingly performed in order to show more manifestly the divinity of Jesus. Miracles wrought on lesser things often effect changes which can be brought about naturally by natural causes (for example, regaining health), but those involving heavenly bodies are both unlike what naturally occurs and not among the deeds of any mere human.

Miracles Wrought on Humans

By far the majority of Christ's miracles that Scripture has recorded involve human beings, which is only as it should be. Christ came into the world to save mankind. "For God sent the Son into the world, not to condemn the world, but that the world might be saved through him" (John 3:17).

When the disciples of John the Baptist come to Jesus and ask the central question, " 'Are you he who is to come, or shall we look for another?' " (Luke 7:19), the answer not only lists the kinds of miracles Jesus performed but once more indicates that he performs them in order that men might know who he is.

"And he answered them, 'Go and tell John what you have seen and heard: the blind receive their sight, the lame walk, lepers are cleansed, and the deaf hear, the dead are raised up, the poor have the good news preached to them' " (Luke 7:22).

HEALINGS — The Gospel accounts of Jesus' healing of the sick begin with Peter's mother-in-law whom Jesus cures of a fever by taking her hand and lifting her up, whereupon she serves him and his disciples. Matthew, Mark, and Luke recount the episode. That same evening, the sick and the possessed are brought to him and he casts out the demons and heals the sick (see Mark 1:32-34 and Luke 4:40-41). Matthew adds that Jesus did this to fulfill the prophecy of Isaiah, " 'He took our infirmities and bore our diseases' " (Matthew 8:17).

This is a power he gave to the Twelve Apostles when he sent them out. "And he called the twelve together and gave them power and authority over all demons and to cure diseases, and he sent them out to preach the kingdom of God and to heal" (Luke 9:1-2). We will consider in the next section the significance of miracles performed by the Apostles.

Often a miraculous healing is thought to be done at an inappropriate time, for example, on the sabbath. "One sabbath when he went to dine at the house of a ruler who belonged to the Pharisees, they were watching him. And behold, there was a man before him who had dropsy. And Jesus spoke to the lawyers and Pharisees, saying, 'Is it lawful to cure on the sabbath, or not?' " (Luke 14:1-3). Receiving no answer, Jesus heals the man, thus indicating that he not only has power to cure but also power over the sabbath.

A healing that Jesus performed when Judas leads the crowd to arrest him is particularly significant. Shortly Jesus will be taunted and mocked, by priests, by soldiers, by the crowd, demanding a miracle, and none will be performed. But just before Jesus allows himself to be taken, he gives this manifestation of his power. "Then Simon Peter, having a sword, drew it and struck the high priest's slave and cut off his right ear. The slave's name was Malchus. Jesus said to Peter, 'Put your sword into its sheath; shall I not drink the cup which the Father has given me?' " (John 18:10-11). John tells us who used the sword, the servant's name, and that it was the right ear that was severed; but he does not tell us of the miracle, as Luke does: "But Jesus said, 'No more of this!' And he touched his ear and healed him" (22:51).

CLEANSING OF LEPERS — The Gospels give us several accounts of Jesus curing leprosy. "And a leper came to him beseeching him, and kneeling said to him, 'If you will, you can make me clean.' Moved with pity, he stretched out his hand and touched him, and said to him, 'I will; be clean.' And immediately the leprosy left him, and he was made clean" (Mark 1:40-42). Simply by willing it, Jesus can with a touch immediately cure this dreadful disease.

In another famous account, the cure of leprosy is made to show that not all are equally grateful for the cleansing. "On the way to Jerusalem he was passing along between Samaria and Galilee. And as he entered a village, he was met by ten lepers, who stood at a distance and lifted up their voices and said, 'Jesus, Master, have mercy on us.' When he saw them he said to them, 'Go and show yourselves to the priests.' And as they went they were cleansed. Then one of them, when he saw that he was healed, turned back, praising God with a loud voice; and he fell on his face at Jesus' feet, giving him thanks. Now he was a Samaritan. Then said Jesus, 'Were not ten cleansed? Where are the nine? Was no one found to return and give praise to God except this foreigner?' And he said to him, 'Rise and go your way; your faith has made you well' " (Luke 17:11-19).

Basic to the account is that Jesus, by willing it, cures ten lepers. That leprosy may also stand for sin and curing for forgiveness is true enough, but this further significance is based on the literal healing. Here, moreover, with the emphasis on the fact that it is a foreigner who thanks God for what has been done to him, there is the suggestion of the universality of Jesus' mission, to Jews, but to gentiles as well. We might wonder if the nine ungrateful ones remained cured, since Jesus tells the Samaritan that it is his faith that has saved him. This suggests that not everyone who is the beneficiary of a miracle acknowledges this. The reference to the Samaritan's faith indicates that he knows his cure was miraculous and therefore that he should praise God for it.

RESTORING SIGHT — If the curing of leprosy with a touch or simply with a word indicates that Jesus has a power that is not human, the restoration of sight to the blind is another deed that can only be miraculous given the way Jesus brings it about. "And they came to Jericho; and as he was leaving Jericho with his disciples and a great multitude, Bartimaeus, a blind beggar, the son of Timaeus, was sitting by the roadside. And when he heard that it was Jesus of Nazareth, he began to cry out and say, 'Jesus, Son of David, have mercy on me!' And many rebuked him, telling him to be silent; but he cried out all the more, 'Son of David, have mercy on me!' And Jesus stopped and said, 'Call him.' And they called the blind man, saying to him, 'Take heart; rise, he is calling you.' And throwing off his mantle, he sprang up and came to Jesus. And Jesus said to him, 'What do you want me to do for you?' And the blind man said to him, 'Master, let me receive my sight.' And Jesus said to him, 'Go your way; your faith has made you well.' And immediately he received his sight and followed him on the way" (Mark 10:46-52).

Earlier Mark recounted another miracle performed on a blind man where the cure is accomplished by degrees. Jesus applies spittle to the man's eyes and asks if he can see. "And he looked up and said, 'I see men; but they look like trees, walking.' Then again he laid his

hands upon his eyes; and he looked intently and was re-
stored, and saw everything clearly'' (Mark 8:24-25).

In another instance when Jesus heals a man born
blind, an occasion is provided to distinguish between such
calamities and sin. Jesus is asked if the man's blindness
is due to his sins or his parents'. Neither, Jesus replies,
pointing out that the afflicted man was born blind in order that the works of God might be manifest in him.
John's account of this miracle (9:1ff) is of particular interest. Jesus anoints the blind man's eyes and tells him
to go wash in the pool of Siloam. He does, and he can see
as a result. Now a drama begins which is instructive as
to the way in which men reacted to Jesus' miracles.

People seeing the man walking along begin to argue
whether it is the same man they have known as a blind
beggar. Some say yes; others say no, he only looks like
him. But the man says that he is. Whereupon he is taken
to the Pharisees. They ask him how he got his sight back,
and he tells them. The first reaction is that anyone who
gives a blind man sight on the sabbath cannot be from
God. But that raises the question of how a sinner could
work such signs. So they ask the former blind man who
he thinks Jesus is. "He is a prophet," he says simply (see
John 9:17).

But skepticism continues that this man was once
blind, so his parents are summoned and questioned: Was
he born blind and if so how come he can see now? " 'We
know that this is our son, and that he was born blind; but
how he now sees we do not know, nor do we know who

opened his eyes. Ask him; he is of age, he will speak for himself' " (John 9:20-21).

So they bring back the man and tell him he has been given sight by a sinner. The man says, " 'Whether he is a sinner, I do not know; one thing I know, that though I was blind, now I see' " (John 9:25). How, the Pharisees press the once-sightless man, did Jesus do it? He has already told them, the man points out, asking if they are curious because they want to become disciples of Jesus. This earns him abuse. The Pharisees know Moses was from God, but they don't know about Jesus. Whereupon the man born blind says, " 'Why, this is a marvel! You do not know where he comes from, and yet he opened my eyes. We know that God does not listen to sinners, but if any one is a worshiper of God and does his will, God listens to him. Never since the world began has it been heard that any one opened the eyes of a man born blind. If this man were not from God, he could do nothing' " (John 9:30-33). Indignant, the Pharisees turn him out.

The Pharisees resist admitting that what has happened has happened since; if they did, they would have to conclude what the man whose sight has been given him concludes. But it becomes progressively harder to deny what has happened, yet the route is always open. It is open precisely because what is said to have happened, cannot have happened, unless. . .

At this point it is easier for the Pharisees to deny it happened than to accept it and to draw the logical conclusion.

But this marvelous chapter of John's Gospel is not yet through. Jesus, hearing what has happened, seeks out the recently blind man and asks: " 'Do you believe in the Son of man [that is, the Son of God]?' He answered, 'And who is he, sir, that I may believe in him?' Jesus said to him, 'You have seen him, and it is he who speaks to you.' He said, 'Lord, I believe'; and he worshiped him" (9:35-38). Jesus then says that he has come into the world in order that the blind might see, and some Pharisees who are there ask if they are also blind. "Jesus said to them, 'If you were blind, you would have no guilt; but now that you say "We see," your guilt remains' " (9:41).

The cured man moves through stages. By accepting what has happened to him as a miracle, he sees it as the work of God. He refuses the suggestion that Jesus is a sinner, because God heard him when he wished to restore the man's sight. The next stage is reached when he accepts Jesus as the Son of God and thus more than a prophet.

This final act of the drama indicates that being in a situation where a miracle has been performed and resisting accepting it can be a culpable act. The Pharisees are willfully resisting what they know they should accept. This suggests that while a miracle does not compel acceptance as an act of God, the refusal to accept it as such can be culpable.

RAISING THE DEAD — To cure diseases is a sign of the power Jesus has. To cure leprosy, even more so. To restore sight or to give sight to one born blind, well, this is extraordinary indeed. The escalation in the manifesting of Jesus' power continues until we confront accounts where he raises the dead to life.

"Soon afterward he went to a city called Nain, and his disciples and a great crowd went with him. As he drew near to the gate of the city, behold, a man who had died was being carried out, the only son of his mother, and she was a widow; and a large crowd from the city was with her. And when the Lord saw her, he had compassion on her and said to her, 'Do not weep.' And he came and touched the bier, and the bearers stood still. And he said, 'Young man, I say to you, arise.' And the dead man sat up, and began to speak. And he gave him to his mother" (Luke 7:11-15).

The witnesses react with fear but then begin to glorify God because of the great prophet who is in their midst. "God has visited his people," they cry.

On another occasion, Jesus is approached by the ruler of a synagogue whose daughter is on the point of death; but as they talk, word comes that the girl is dead. Jesus says to the ruler, "Do not fear, only believe," and he offers to go home with him. "When they came to the house of the ruler of the synagogue, he saw a tumult, and people weeping and wailing loudly. And when he had entered, he said to them, 'Why do you make a tumult and weep? The child is not dead but sleeping.' And they laughed at him. But he put them all outside, and took the child's father and mother and those who were with him, and went in where the child was. Taking her by the hand he said to her, 'Talitha cumi'; which means, 'Little girl, I say to you, arise.' And immediately the girl got up and walked; for she was twelve years old. And immediately they were overcome with amazement" (Mark 5:38-42).

The son of the widow was recently dead; the daughter of the ruler had just died. But the raising of Lazarus takes place days after the man's death. It is as if even here in these cases of the raising of the dead the miracle becomes more and more striking.

The raising of Lazarus is told only by John, and it is a lengthy account, taking up almost the whole of Chapter 11. Lazarus, the brother of Martha and Mary, falls ill and dies in Bethany; Jesus hears of it and goes to them, arriving four days after Lazarus died. Martha says to Jesus that she knows Lazarus would not have died if Jesus had been there and that even now God will grant Jesus whatever he asks.

"Jesus said to her, 'Your brother will rise again.' Martha said to him, 'I know that he will rise again in the resurrection at the last day.' Jesus said to her, 'I am the resurrection and the life; he who believes in me, though he die, yet shall he live, and whoever lives and believes in me shall never die. Do you believe this?' She said to him, 'Yes, Lord; I believe that you are the Christ, the Son of God, he who is coming into the world' '' (11:23-27). It is then Mary's turn to tell Jesus if only he had been there her brother would not have died, and Jesus asks where they have laid Lazarus. He is taken to the place of burial, where he weeps; as Jesus mourns Lazarus, he is asked why he could not have saved his friend from death when he has given sight to the blind.

In response, Jesus orders the stone to be taken away from the tomb and Martha remarks that after four days Lazarus will already have decayed. Jesus chides her and the stone is removed. "And Jesus lifted up his eyes and said, 'Father, I thank thee that thou hast heard me. I knew that thou hearest me always, but I have said this on account of the people standing by, that they may believe that thou didst send me.' When he had said this, he cried with a loud voice, 'Lazarus, come out.' The dead man came out, his hands and feet bound with bandages, and his face wrapped with a cloth. Jesus said to them, 'Unbind him, and let him go' '' (11:41-44).

That scene, beloved of painters, stays in the mind. We easily think that if we had been there, only one reaction would have been possible. Yet John says that many, not all, who saw what Jesus had done, believed in him. Others went away to report him to the Pharisees.

Miracles Wrought on Lesser Things

The fourth class of miracles wrought by Jesus, those performed on irrational creatures, completes the manifestation of his power, showing the whole of nature to be subject to him.

"And when he had ceased speaking, he said to Simon, 'Put out into the deep and let down your nets for a catch.' And Simon answered, 'Master, we toiled all night and

took nothing! But at your word I will let down the nets.'
And when they had done this, they enclosed a great shoal
of fish; and as their nets were breaking, they beckoned to
their partners in the other boat to come and help them.
And they came and filled both the boats, so that they began to sink. But when Simon Peter saw it, he fell down at
Jesus' knees, saying, 'Depart from me, for I am a sinful
man, O Lord' '' (Luke 5:4-8).

It is as a result of this miracle that Simon and others
leave their boats and follow Jesus who tells them he will
make them fishers of men.

A not dissimilar miracle occurs when Jesus and his
friends are in a boat and a storm comes up. "And when
he got into the boat, his disciples followed him. And
behold, there arose a great storm on the sea, so that the
boat was being swamped by the waves; but he was
asleep. And they went and woke him, saying, 'Save us,
Lord; we are perishing.' And he said to them, 'Why are
you afraid, O men of little faith?' Then he rose and rebuked the winds and the sea; and there was a great calm.
And the men marveled, saying, 'What sort of man is this,
that even the winds and sea obey him?' '' (Matthew
8:23-27).

Another miracle which manifests Jesus' power over
the elements also involves the lake. "When evening
came, his disciples went down to the sea, got into a boat,
and started across the sea to Capernaum. It was now
dark, and Jesus had not yet come to them. The sea rose
because a strong wind was blowing. When they had

rowed about three or four miles, they saw Jesus walking on the sea and drawing near to the boat. They were frightened, but he said to them, 'It is I; do not be afraid.' Then they were glad to take him into the boat, and immediately the boat was at the land to which they were going" (John 6:16-21).

Finally, there is the great miracle of the loaves and fishes. "In those days, when again a great crowd had gathered, and they had nothing to eat, he called his disciples to him, and said to them, 'I have compassion on the crowd, because they have been with me now three days, and have nothing to eat; and if I send them away hungry to their homes, they will faint on the way; and some of them have come a long way.' And his disciples answered him, 'How can one feed these men with bread here in a desert?' And he asked them, 'How many loaves have you?' They said, 'Seven.' And he commanded the crowd to sit down on the ground; and he took the seven loaves, and having given thanks he broke them and gave them to his disciples to set before the people; and they set them before the crowd. And they had a few small fish; and having blessed them, he commanded that these also should be set before them. And they ate, and were satisfied; and they took up the broken pieces left over, seven baskets full. And there were about four thousand people" (Mark 8:1-9).

In the four types of miracles, then, Jesus shows himself to be in possession of a power that can only be called divine. In these episodes, he himself is depicted as look-

ing like a man among men, but what he does is not doable
by mere men. There is another episode in the Gospels in
which Jesus shows himself in his glory, transfigured.
"And after six days Jesus took with him Peter and James
and John his brother, and led them up a high mountain
apart. And he was transfigured before them, and his face
shone like the sun, and his garments became white as
light. And behold, there appeared to them Moses and Elijah, talking with him. And Peter said to Jesus, 'Lord, it is
well that we are here; if you wish, I will make three
booths here, one for you and one for Moses and one for
Elijah.' He was still speaking, when lo, a bright cloud
overshadowed them, and a voice from the cloud said,
'This is my beloved Son, with whom I am well pleased;
listen to him.' When the disciples heard this, they fell on
their faces, and were filled with awe. But Jesus came
and touched them, saying, 'Rise, and have no fear.' And
when they lifted up their eyes, they saw no one but Jesus
only" (Matthew 17:1-8).

When Jesus was baptized by John the Baptist there
was a similar heavenly endorsement of him. "And when
he came up out of the water, immediately he saw the
heavens opened and the Spirit descending upon him like a
dove; and a voice came from heaven, 'Thou art my
beloved Son, with thee I am well pleased'" (Mark
1:10-11). In the transfiguration of our Lord, the presence
of Moses and Elijah is taken to indicate that Jesus re-
deems not only those who come after him, like Peter and
James and John, but also his historical predecessors.

The Resurrection

No account of the miracles of Jesus can exclude the event that more than any other thing makes clear the divinity of Jesus: his resurrection.

In the liturgical year, the season of Lent prepares us for the annual recalling of the passion of our Lord, the forty days recalling the period when Jesus withdrew into the desert. In the final fortnight of Lent, the narratives of the passion remind us of the horrors of Christ's condemnation, the scourging at the pillar and crowning of thorns, the *via crucis*, and finally the crucifixion itself. The public ministry of Jesus thus appears to end in ignominy and failure. And so it truly would have if the event he had foretold to his disciples — for example, at the transfiguration — did not cast the whole thing in a new light. Having been executed and buried, Christ rises from the dead.

The Gospel of St. Mark narrates Jesus' resurrection and ascension in its final chapter. The Sunday after the crucifixion, Mary Magdalene and Mary the mother of James, and another woman, Salome, go to the grave of Jesus to anoint the body. They find the stone rolled back, the grave empty, and a young man in white who tells them Jesus of Nazareth is not there and that they should go tell the disciples and Peter. Then Jesus appears to Mary Magdalene, and she tells the others. "But when they heard that he was alive and had been seen by her, they would not believe it" (Mark 16:11).

In Matthew, the encounter with Jesus is put as follows: "Now after the sabbath, toward the dawn of the first of the week, Mary Magdalene and the other Mary went to see the sepulchre. And behold, there was a great earthquake; for an angel of the Lord descended from heaven and came and rolled back the stone, and sat upon it. His appearance was like lightning, and his raiment white as snow. And for fear of him the guards trembled and became like dead men. But the angel said to the women, 'Do not be afraid; for I know that you seek Jesus who was crucified. He is not here; for he has risen, as he said. Come, see the place where he lay. Then go quickly and tell his disciples that he has risen. . . .' And behold, Jesus met them and said, 'Hail!' And they came up and took hold of his feet and worshiped him" (Matthew 28:1-9).

Thus does triumph emerge from apparent tragedy and loss. Jesus who had been most cruelly crucified — and most certainly lifeless — rises from the dead. This conquest of death on Jesus' part is a promise of our own future condition. Without belief in Christ's resurrection, the story of the Gospels would be foolish. "If Christ be not risen, our faith is in vain" (see 1 Corinthians 15:14).

The resurrection, then, would seem to be the supreme manifestation of Christ's divine power.

✳ ✳ ✳

This chapter has had as its purpose to put before us the range and kinds of miracles attributed to Jesus in the Gospel accounts. As often as not, these accounts themselves make clear the purpose of the miracle. But a good many questions arise with respect to such events, and it is to those questions that we will turn in the third part of this study. A rather obvious question that arises is: How could someone witness a miracle and fail to believe that Jesus is what he claimed to be? And yet, as the narratives make clear, not all witnesses of miracles believed in Jesus. That question and others will occupy us later.

CHAPTER THREE

Miracles of the Apostles

Already in the Gospel accounts, Jesus sends out his followers to preach and to perform wonders, to heal, cast out demons, and the like. On one occasion, they ask him why they were unable to drive out an unclean spirit and are told that there are some that can only be expelled after much prayer and fasting.

But it is, appropriately enough, in the Acts of the Apostles, that we are given quite detailed accounts of miracles and wonders performed by the Apostles. Acts begins with our Lord's ascension and then Pentecost and the account of Peter's sermon which is heard by different people in their own tongues. The sermon is also notable for the way in which Peter shows that in Jesus were the Scriptures fulfilled. He also reminds them of the miracles and wonders Jesus performed among them, signs God did in him. This Jesus, he tells them, is risen from the dead. Some three thousand are converted.

When Peter cures a lame man at the temple gate, he is quite explicit as to the source of his ability to do so. "But Peter said, 'I have no silver and gold, but I give you what I have; in the name of Jesus Christ of Nazareth, walk.' And he took him by the right hand and raised him up; and immediately his feet and ankles were made strong. And leaping up he stood and walked and entered the temple with them, walking and leaping and praising God" (Acts 3:6-8). The miracle provides the occasion of an interrogation by the high priest, and mention is made of how remarkable it is that these simple and illiterate followers of Jesus now speak with learning and authority.

Acts mentions, without specifying them, many signs and wonders wrought by the Apostles (5:12), thus making it clear that those that are described are but a sample. The Apostles are put in prison, but prisons cannot hold them. Stephen, chosen to replace Judas, performs many signs and wonders (6:8) but then is stoned to death. Peter raises Tabitha to life. "But Peter put them all outside and knelt down and prayed; then turning to the body he said, 'Tabitha, rise.' And she opened her eyes, and when she saw Peter she sat up" (9:40).

Acts is studded with accounts of apostolic miracles, among them Peter's deliverance from prison (as described in Chapter 12) and Paul curing a cripple and doing other wonders — "And God did extraordinary mir-

acles by the hands of Paul" (19:11). Paul too raises the
dead to life, as in Chapter 20 where we read that a young
man named Eutychus, sitting in a window, nods off while
Paul preaches and falls to his death. Paul goes down, em-
braces the body, and assures the others that his soul is in
him. "And they took the lad away alive, and were not a
little comforted" (20:12).

The point of the miracles performed by the Apostles
is to establish their authority and to serve as proof of the
message they bring. They do not do these things in their
own name, but by invoking the power of Jesus.

From beginning to end, the Scriptures are full of
stories of signs and wonders, manifestations of the divine
power. Without them, the sacred books would be radically other than they are. Doubtless, signs and wonders play
different roles in the Old and New Testaments, but the
link between the Old and the New, connects the miracles
as well.

Revelation is completed with Holy Scripture, but
signs and wonders — and indeed private revelations —
continue even to our own time. Let us turn now to the
way in which those supernatural events, the wonderful
and miraculous, play a role in the life of Christians down
the ages.

PART TWO
Miracles in the
Life of the Church

Prologue

We have set before ourselves something of the richness and variety of the signs and wonders recorded in the Scriptures which show forth the power of God, whether through the prophets, the miracles of Jesus, or the wonders worked by the Apostles after our Lord's ascension into heaven. Various and numerous as these are, they nonetheless have at least the unity of being found in the same source. Now we shift our attention to an area which is considerably harder to lay hold of.

There is a tendency among historians — that is, social historians — to seek the "people's" history as opposed to the history of institutions and of the functionaries of institutions. In the case of Church history, this can take the form of looking for an almost underground church which is thought to be insufficiently if at all accounted for by the history of the official Church. I do not have in mind any such distinction as that when I separate Part 2 from Part 3 of this book, where I will consider what theologians and the magisterium have to say about miracles.

The biblical stories were put before the mind and imagination of a simple and generally illiterate faithful by means of the liturgy and sermons but even more vividly in stone and glass and bronze. The windows of Chartres and of the Ste.-Chapelle, the baptistry doors in Florence, for example, are the means whereby ordinary people became saturated with the Bible. Prior to printing, and indeed afterward, the cost of a book was enormous and of course few beyond the clerical order were capable of reading them in any case. Expensive books were chained in place, Bibles among them; but we must not think of this as an effort to conceal the Scriptures, lest people discover the truth and overthrow the hierarchy. If the stained-glass windows, the statues, those bronze doors, and the like function somewhat as comic books do today, the elegant gilt books chained to their reading stands are not unlike our coffee-table items. Not your workaday book even for the literate. The exquisite Books of Hours to be seen in the Vatican Library and in El Escorial, for example, seldom have a dog-eared look about them. Not only would one need the eye of an eagle to read the text, but the paintings, the stylized capital letters, and the illuminations, among other elements, make such items works of art to be marveled at rather than prayed with.

We can of course distinguish between the worship and devotion of the Church liturgy, the seasons of the year, the calendar of the saints, such processions as those of Corpus Christi, and merely private devotions. The Church at prayer — the *ecclesia orans*, monks and canons reciting the Divine Office in monastery and cathedral — is another instance of what we may call the official and public worship of the Church. The text is set, the priest is the minister whose words and gestures are not expressions of private devotion but those of the lieutenant of the people and of the Lord. The priest is the bridge, the pontifex, between God and man. Private devotions are often very closely linked to this public and liturgical worship. A saint has his day in the calendar but may also be the patron of a place or church and be invoked regularly. There may be relics of him there which are venerated, not just publicly and officially, but privately and spontaneously. Devotion to the Mother of God is of particular importance here.

Indeed, what we are after in this part could be illustrated in terms of Marian devotion alone: Mary's liturgical feasts, the hymns and prayers of her office, such devotions as the rosary, churches and places named after her, shrines which commemorate her life (for example, the House of Loreto), her miracles, her appearances. And there is the way she is depicted in religious art across the ages, the poems and stories in which she is featured as worker of wonders to those who seek her intercession. And indeed in this part we shall be drawing attention to many Marian features of the devotional practices of Christians over the ages. But we shall not confine ourselves to these.

The division I have hit upon — and any number of others might have done, indeed might have done better — is this:

✓ Pilgrimages and Shrines.
✓ Relics and Uncorrupted Bodies.
✓ Apparitions of Mary.

————————————————

CHAPTER FOUR

Pilgrimages and Shrines

THE HOLY LAND — A first object of pilgrimage in the Christian era is the Holy Land, the land of the Bible, where the places marking the great events in the life of Christ were early identified. Unless this devout desire is understood, the fervor with which the Crusades of the Middle Ages were undertaken will never be understood. And of course to this day it can be the high point in one's life to go to Israel, to visit Bethlehem, Nazareth, Jerusalem; to see the site of Mary's visit to Elizabeth, the Mount of Transfiguration, the Garden of Gethsemani, the Holy Sepulcher, and the spot from which Jesus rose into heaven. What a profound experience to visit the Mount of the Beatitudes and Cana where Christ worked his first miracle!

Nowadays each of these is well marked, with appropriate biblical passages mounted. For example, the Magnificat, in the Latin of the Vulgate as well as other languages, marks the place of the Visitation. It is after the year 313 that the Holy Land achieves prominence as a place of pilgrimage, thanks to Constantine, to his mother (St. Helena), and to St. Jerome, who settled there and undertook the translation which becomes the Vulgate. Indeed, St. Helena's discovery of the true cross is a major item in her life. She brought many things back to Rome — for example, the *scala santa*, which pilgrims ascend on their knees. These are the stairs Jesus mounted to be condemned by Pilate. They are found in the same square as St. John Lateran in Rome. One often hears it wryly said that if all the pieces of the true cross were assembled they would in the aggregate make something many times larger than Christ's cross could have been. As it happens, this charge is simply false. See Evelyn Waugh's novel *Helena*. Perhaps such remarks do not arise from skepticism; rather, they arise from a kind of doubt that one is actually in the presence of wood from that cross, or on the very spot where the resurrection occurred, or kneeling where Christ wept over Jerusalem. Perhaps we would be more comfortable if we thought all such physical things had vaporized and that we should not seek out those precise coordinates of space where Christ lived out his life.

The desire to make pilgrimages to such sites, like the desire to collect relics of the saints, is an extension of the incarnational nature of Christianity. The Second Person of the Trinity became man, was born as a child, in a very definite place, at a very definite time. Christ walked and talked and performed wonders on days not unlike those that make up our own lives. To seek out the places where he lived is to acknowledge that awful truth of our faith: God became man. The physical world can never be the same after that, but it is by acknowledging that our faith encompasses claims about places and times of a quite definite sort that we accept fully its essential mystery. Otherwise, Christ may become an anonymous someone who lived somewhere or other but has now surmounted such limitations. Of course the risen Christ is different. But let us not think that the desire to be where Christ was is somehow irrelevant.

It is Eusebius who provides us with information on early pilgrimages to the Holy Land, and indeed tells us of Constantine and his mother. The finding of the Holy Sepulcher and the erection of a basilica on the site is attributed to Constantine; Eusebius tells us it was Helena who built basilicas over the sites of our Lord's nativity and ascension. Others mention that St. Helena found the true cross; that St. Jerome lived in the Holy Land for thirty years, undertaking his great effort to establish the text of the Bible and to put it into Latin, and also influencing a number of women to come there and to establish monasteries. "Just as one understands the Greek historians better when one has seen Athens," Jerome wrote, "or the third book of Virgil when one has sailed to Troas or Sicily, so too we understand Scripture better when we have seen Judea with our own eyes and discovered what still remains of ancient towns. That is why I myself took care to travel through this land." Soon it had become a common meeting place for Christians from around the known world, where one might meet visitors from Gaul and Britain, Armenia and Persia, India, Ethiopia, and Egypt. All were there to enter where Christ was buried, to kiss the wood of the cross, to climb the Mount of Olives and, in the other holy places, to meditate on the events of Christ's life.

THE HOLY CITY — Gradually, Rome too became an object of pilgrimage. Christians wanted to see the catacombs, where Peter and Paul were buried, and the Coliseum where so many had been martyred. If the Holy Land provided sites of both the Old and New Testaments, Rome included both the pagan past and memorials to the gradual ascendency of Christianity. The churches and basilicas, the art, the restorations — all obeying the rhythm of history as the fortunes of the city waxed and waned (Gibbon reflected on the sheep that wandered where the mighty once had trod) — the papacy, and, increasingly, the Vatican and St. Peter's, took their place in the mental geography of the Christian. Luther came to Rome on a memorable visit, entering the Piazza del Popolo, and found the city less than edifying. But Rome is indeed a holy city, sanctified by the blood of martyrs and of saints over the centuries, some of them popes.

In these times of affluence and cheap travel, the numbers who visit Rome each year are astronomical, and many are there at least partly for purposes of pilgrimage. The pope has become a must of the tour, a public figure to increasingly larger crowds, with almost tragic consequences in the case of Pope John Paul II in 1981, when an attempt on his life was made. The Catholic wants to see the bishop of Rome, the successor of Peter, the vicar of Christ on earth. And in recent years the tomb of St. Peter far beneath the Renaissance basilica has been made available for restricted visits. Near the Forum, one can visit the cell where Peter and Paul were imprisoned and where a fountain of water sprang up miraculously and still flows. And there are other objects of pilgrimage in the Holy City that I will mention later.

From the year 313, when Constantine built a basilica over the tomb of Peter on the Vatican hill, and then St. John Lateran and St. Paul's Outside-the-Walls and St. Agnes and the catacombs began to receive proper care, the pilgrims began to arrive, along the Via Aurelia, the Via Ostiensis, and the Via Appia. The sack of Rome by the Vandals did not end the practice.

Why did the pilgrims come? To visit the sites, to be sure, but also to take home relics — from the catacombs, a link from the chain of Peter, a bit of the true cross. We are told that collecting bones was a later custom. There are warnings about all this, of course, warnings against superstition, but that is an abuse of the practice. When engaged in with spiritual profit, these visits and mementos of the visits provided vivid reminders of the Christian life and its demands. In Trastevere, the church of St.

Mary and a hostel were built for Anglo-Saxon pilgrims, and pilgrims from Ireland seemed to be everywhere. Indeed, to go on pilgrimage "for the love of God" became a national trait.

Guidebooks for pilgrims to Rome have come down to us from early times, and scholars find them an exciting mixture of fact and legend. On the roads to Rome, guesthouses sprang up, providing overnight accommodation. The Church declared Holy Years as early as the fourteenth century and the custom evolved to the present system where they occur every twenty-five years.

Another early object of pilgrimage was the tomb of St. Martin of Tours in Gaul. From the late fourth century the pilgrims come and St. Gregory of Tours, two centuries later, speaks of the unceasing stream of pilgrims to his predecessor's tomb. But one that will be particularly familiar is that to Canterbury.

CANTERBURY TALES — Chaucer's classic is so familiar that it can have the effect of obscuring why it was that all his motley crew were on their way to Canterbury. Not that he does not say, as the following so aptly puts it:

> *When April with his showers sweet with fruit*
> *The drought of March has pierced unto the root*
> *And bathed each vein with liquor that has*
> *   power*
> *To generate therein and sire the flower. . .*
> *Then do folk long to go on pilgrimage.*

He makes it sound like spring fever, but the purpose is finally expressed:

And specially from every shire's end
Of England they to Canterbury wend,
The holy blessed martyr there to seek
Who helped them when they lay so ill and
weak.

Thomas à Becket was murdered in his cathedral at Canterbury on December 29, 1170, and in the next fifteen years there were over seven hundred recorded miracles attributed to him. Quite soon the site of his martyrdom rivaled the Holy Land and Rome as a place of international pilgrimage. The number of early miracles is not a guess, since two monks, Benedict and William, had the task of recording them from 1171 to 1184. Both men had been present in the cathedral the night Thomas was martyred. Stained-glass windows in the Trinity Chapel of the cathedral depict some miracles of St. Thomas. Sister Benedicta Ward, in her discussion of Canterbury in *Miracles and the Medieval Mind* (University of Pennsylvania Press, 1982), noting that the records show more rich people than poor people being cured, observes that the poor could not afford an offering and thus did not announce a miracle until they were free of the church and the recording monk. The basis for her observation is a remark of the recording monk in the records themselves. The monks did not accept all claims that miracles had occurred, to the dismay of the claimants. John of Salisbury, a very learned and sophisticated man, gave powerful testimony to the efficacy of St. Thomas of Canterbury.

"In the place where Thomas suffered, and where he lay the night through, before the high altar awaiting burial and where he was buried at last, the palsied are cured, the blind see, the deaf hear, the dumb speak, the lepers are cleansed, those possessed of a devil are freed, and the sick are made whole from all manner of disease, blasphemers taken over by the devil are put to confusion." And then he adds, "I should not have dreamt of writing such words on any account had not my eyes been witness to the certainty of this."

St. Thomas was canonized by Pope Alexander III just three years after the murder in the cathedral. The Holy Father ordered that the body be enshrined and that the day of St. Thomas's death be annually observed. A Mass and Office of St. Thomas of Canterbury were observed in the universal Church. With canonization and full liturgical honors, the official Church and popular devotion fuse. Asking the saints to intercede on behalf of the Church militant to obtain spiritual and material favors is of course mainstream Christian devotion. Pilgrimages are outgrowths of this. They involve, needless to say, a good deal of local pride and regional loyalty. But in the case of St. Thomas of Canterbury, as in that of St. Martin of Tours, the devotion is international and their shrines deserve to be compared with Rome and the lands of the Bible.

ST. JAMES OF COMPOSTELA — Another world-class shrine deserving of mention is the tomb of the Apostle James located at Compostela in northern Spain. The Rue

St.-Jacques in Paris is so-called because it was by that street that pilgrims left Paris to set off for Santiago de Compostela. There was a hospice in Paris where pilgrims from the north, from Flanders and Wallonia and elsewhere, stayed before continuing on to Spain. They attended Mass at St.-Jacques-de-la-Boucherie and then, crossing the Seine by the Petit-Pont, continued up the Rue St.-Jacques.

There was a guide for pilgrims to Compostela which makes up the fifth book of the life of St. James (*Liber Sancti Jacobi*), a guide of which we have a separate modern edition. Another book in the original work dealt with the miracles of St. James. These were not all performed at the shrine itself and they favored men and military men at that. St. James was the patron of Spain in driving out the Moors and it was to his shrine that Ferdinand and Isabella came in 1492 to give thanks for the regaining of the country for Christendom.

The guidebook for pilgrims to the shrine tells of the principal routes that will take one there, the names of cities and towns along the way, the three best hospices, the names of those who have made improvements in the route, the good and bad rivers one will encounter, the types of land and peoples along the way, the bodies of saints that can be visited by pilgrims, and then the city and church of St. James itself. The description of the shrine as well as a rather detailed account of the church makes up the bulk of the guidebook.

While some pilgrims, particularly in earlier times,

were doing penance for their sins, and indeed murderers were sometimes sent on a pilgrimage that would take them years, most pilgrims acted out of simple piety and with an eye to spiritual advancement or material advantage. The medieval pilgrim wore special garb, a broad-brimmed hat, a wallet, and a pilgrim's staff. He would receive a blessing before setting off and put his affairs in order. This was not a matter of jetting off for ten days or two weeks and then back to the rat race. A pilgrimage to the Holy Land, to Rome, or to Compostela would not be undertaken lightly. Nor of course would the pilgrim set out alone. Chaucer has taught us to think of bands of pilgrims and so it was. Certain orders were founded to help and protect pilgrims — for example, the Knights of St. James in Spain, the Knights Templars, and even the Knights of Malta.

Shrines were soon festooned with plaques and other ex-voto offerings attesting to some favor or even miracle received; offerings of wax and oil, or perhaps of money, might be made. Confession and the reception of communion at the shrine would be the culmination of the visit. Different emblems were brought back to show that one had indeed reached the goal of the pilgrimage; some examples include a conch-shell emblem for Santiago de Compostela, a replica of Veronica's veil for Rome, and palms from the Holy Land.

This sampling of pilgrimages in early and medieval times could be added to almost indefinitely by mentioning more local shrines. There are shrines that thrive and then die out; there is a waxing and waning in others. Just as the Church constantly puts new models of Christian life before us — canonizing saints whose lives, having been lived nearer in time to us, may speak more directly to us — so we may conjecture that shrines and pilgrimages may play a role in a given time and then speak less to later generations. But the ones I have singled out for mention are shrines to which pilgrims continue to go today.

CHAPTER FIVE

Relics and Uncorrupted Bodies

The Christian belief in the resurrection of the dead is one of the bases for the veneration shown the mortal remains of any person, but this is particularly the case with the saints. The case of St. Polycarp of Smyrna is often cited as a first dramatic instance of the public veneration of the body of a holy person.

During the great persecutions, the bodies of martyrs were collected and buried. Even the instruments of martyrdom were venerated. The underlying reason, theologians like St. John Damascene insisted, is that such veneration is a way of praising God who has raised the venerated to holiness.

Needless to say, one of the chief reasons for wanting relics and for venerating them was to obtain the intercession of the saint involved. It is when such favors are received and acknowledged that petition changes to thanksgiving and, again, the thanks are due chiefly to God. Relics became objects of booty, as during the Crusades, and of commerce as well. Obviously, there were many opportunities for abuse, and abuses there were. But in practice and in theory, the veneration of relics is an integral part of Christianity.

Tastes differ, of course. A visitor to the Capuchin church on the Via Veneto in Rome, where the bones of dead monks are arranged in rather gruesome designs in a series of side altars, may be put in mind of a charnel house rather than a place of worship; here the *memento mori* has been carried to ridiculous extremes. Or are we put off by it in a way that would not bear up under close scrutiny?

In Alba de Tormes, in Spain, not far from Salamanca, one can see in reliquaries the arm bone and heart of St. Theresa of Ávila and, across the square, the writing finger of St. John of the Cross. When St. Thomas Aquinas died in Fossanova, Italy, his erstwhile colleagues at the University of Paris put in an urgent — and unsuccessful — request that his body be brought back to them for veneration. The heart of St. Vincent de Paul is enshrined in a side altar in the Rue du Bac in Paris. One could go on.

During the Reformation, there was a great deal of scolding about the custom of pilgrimages and the veneration of relics. Erasmus was particularly disapproving. During the Enlightenment there was a dismissal of such practices as superstition, and when the French Revolution came many shrines and relics were destroyed. There is a type of mind that cannot bear the thought that the supernatural exists and that it can get mixed up in the ordinary things of daily life. Such a mentality has to ignore quite a number of things.

Think, for example, of the Shroud of Turin. Venerated as the burial cloth of Christ on which the imprint of his body was retained, this must have seemed the height of nonsense to the enlightened mind. Those who refuse to find an intimation of the Creator in the world around them are going to be particularly indignant at the suggestion that strange and wondrous items are signs of the special work of God. Surely advances in science should enable one to show scientifically that the shroud is a fraud. It seems that the more tests that are made the more difficult it becomes to dismiss the shroud as some monkish fabrication intended to bilk the simple faithful.

In Naples twice a year the blood of St. Januarius liquefies and you can divide people into two classes as soon as the subject is mentioned. First, there are those who know such things cannot happen and are interested in the event only to the degree of wondering how the priests do it. On the other hand, there are those who know there are more things in heaven and earth than are dreamt of in our philosophy and who might wonder if this is indeed an authentic miracle.

The relics of the saints have effected cures over the centuries, indeed such cures figure regularly in the canonization processes. These are not the superstitious beliefs of the uninstructed and simple faithful, but the solemn acceptance by the Church of the fact that God has worked marvels through his chosen ones.

One of the most striking examples of things impossible to ignore and difficult if not impossible to dismiss is the large number of bodies of saintly persons that have remained incorrupt, sometimes for centuries. Even Catholics may not know of these. Consequently, I want to say something about them in this section.

I mentioned in my introduction that while I was working on this book, I paid a visit to Nevers, France, to the Convent of St.-Gildard. It was a February day; I left Paris by the Gare de Lyon and, after a few hours of travel through a countryside lightly dusted with snow, got off at Nevers. A block from the station, I stopped in a store and asked directions to the shrine of St. Bernadette and, after a short walk, I turned in at the gate of the convent. I proceeded to an open courtyard with the church ahead of me, a museum to the left where mementos could be bought, and on the right a replica of the grotto at Lourdes where Mary had appeared to Bernadette Soubirous in 1858. I crossed to the church and went in and almost immediately my eye went to the shrine.

Bernadette, strikingly beautiful in a glass coffin, her body turned slightly to one side, a rosary in her hands, lies there as though asleep. She died on April 16, 1879. This was February of 1986, when I knelt and prayed and shortly afterward there was a noon Mass that I attended.

My eye kept going back to that preserved body. It gives one pause. A fluke? One reads of caves in Sicily where the dead are buried and something in the atmosphere preserves them all from corruption. Think of the pharaohs. Think of Lenin in Moscow. Of course, the pharaohs and Lenin were mummified, and the caves of Sicily are what they are, apparently indiscriminate in preserving all the bodies. Nevers is not famous for mummified bodies. And Bernadette was a visionary to whom the Blessed Virgin appeared. The connection between that and her incorrupt body seems unavoidable.

It is interesting to note that she has not been lying in that glass coffin in the convent church since 1879. The body was thrice buried and thrice exhumed. Buried shortly after Bernadette's death, on April 19, 1879, the body was first exhumed on September 22, 1909. This was done because her cause had been introduced and a preliminary investigation of her life, virtue, and miracles made. The fact that the body was examined indicates that preservation from corruption is taken to be a sign of saintliness. The examination was made in a quite official way. Present was the bishop of Nevers and more than three witnesses (including the mother superior of the order, two doctors, two stonemasons and two carpenters, the mayor and deputy mayor), all of whom took an oath to tell the truth about what they would find.

Bernadette had been buried in the crypt beneath the chapel of St. Joseph. The coffin was brought up and carried to a room and placed on trestles, the outer wooden coffin unscrewed and the inner lead coffin cut open. The body of Bernadette was in a state of perfect preservation. "The coffin was opened in the presence of the Bishop of Nevers, the mayor of the town, his principal deputy, several canons and ourselves. [The doctors are writing the report.] We noticed no smell. The body was clothed in the habit of Bernadette's order. The habit was damp. Only the face, hands and forearms were uncovered. The head was tilted to the left. The face was dull white. The skin clung to the muscles and the muscles adhered to the bones. The sockets of the eyes were covered by the eyelids. The brows were flat on the skin and stuck to the arches above the eyes. The lashes of the right eyelid were stuck to the skin. The nose was dilated and shrunken. The mouth was slightly open and it could be seen that the teeth were still in place. The hands, which were crossed on her breast, were perfectly preserved, as were the nails. The hands still held a rusting rosary. The veins on the forearms stood out."

The body was washed, clothed, and placed in a new coffin lined with zinc and padded with white silk. The double coffin was closed, soldered, screwed down, sealed, and reburied in the vault.

In August 1913, Pope Pius X declared Bernadette venerable, authorizing the introduction of her cause for beatification and canonization. The First World War delayed matters and it was not until August 3, 1919 that another identification of the body was made. It was still preserved. On April 18, 1925, the body was exhumed again for the removal of relics. As on the first and second occasions, official reports were written. That of Dr. Comte is particularly detailed.

Exposure to the air during these exhumations darkened the skin, and the face and hands as one sees them now are covered with a light film of wax.

You might think that a phenomenon like that — a body of someone who died over a century ago, lying there uncorrupted — would be a hot news item, that people would head for Nevers if only out of curiosity. Pilgrims do come, and in numbers, but most people have no idea that St. Bernadette's incorrupt body is there to be seen. Perhaps you never heard of it before. More amazing than the fact, perhaps, is that Bernadette's body is only one of many that have been preserved intact.

I mentioned earlier that the heart of St. Vincent de Paul can be seen enshrined in a reliquary in a church on the Rue du Bac in Paris. In that same church you can see the uncorrupted body of St. Catherine Labouré, a Daughter of Charity to whom the Blessed Mother appeared several times, once to present her with the Miraculous Medal. All this happened in 1830. Catherine died in 1876. Her body was disinterred in 1930 when she was beatified and found to be intact. You may see it lying beneath the altar of the Blessed Virgin, behind glass, in the chapel of the Daughters of Charity on the Rue du Bac in Paris. I have never been in this chapel when it was not crowded and the devotion of the people is palpable. Over the main altar is a representation of Mary as she appears on the

Miraculous Medal and the legend, "Mary conceived without sin, pray for us who have recourse to thee." Mary is depicted as the Immaculate Conception, the title she gave herself when she appeared to Bernadette.

Bernadette and Catherine died within a few years of each other. Both were blessed with appearances of our Blessed Mother. Both were French. Both lived in the nineteenth century. Another thing they have in common is that I am one of thousands who have been privileged to have seen both their bodies, even though there are many other bodies which have been preserved from corruption.

Another preserved body that I have seen with my own eyes is that of St. Rose of Viterbo. There is also St. Rita of Cascia. She died in 1457 at the age of seventy-six and was not canonized until 1900, but from the time of her death extraordinary things happened. A wonderfully sweet odor emanated from her lifeless body and many miracles were attributed to her.

CHAPTER SIX

Apparitions of Mary

The place of Mary, the Mother of God, in the economy of salvation was made clear by the Fathers of Vatican II in the "Dogmatic Constitution on the Church," called by its opening words *Lumen Gentium*. This remarkable document begins with a discussion of the mystery of the Church, goes on to speak of the people of God, the hierarchical constitution of the Church, the role of the laity, the universal call to holiness, the religious life, eschatology, and — by way of culmination, in its final chapter — discusses the Blessed Virgin Mary, Mother of God, in the mystery of Christ and the Church.

It is because he wills the redemption of the whole world that God sent his only begotten Son, born of a Virgin, that we might become adopted children. The mystery of this salvation is both revealed and continued by the Church in which the faithful adhere to Christ as to their head, commemorating and venerating all the holy saints, and, in the first place, Mary the Virgin Mother of God.

It was to Mary that the angel appeared, asking her to participate in God's plan and become the Virgin Mother of his Son by the power of the Holy Spirit. The Mother of Jesus, she is also the mother of all his adopted brethren. Christ on the cross gave her to us as our mother and through the centuries she participates in the redeeming mission of the Church. Mary occupies in the Church the highest place, next to Christ himself and closest to him. She is the mother of the Church. We are urged to remember that true devotion to Mary does not consist in sterile and fugitive emotion nor in empty credulity, but proceeds from true faith, whereby we are led to recognize the excellence of the Mother of God and are stirred to filial love toward Mary our mother and to the imitation of her virtues.

It is mainstream official Catholic doctrine that Mary is at the very center of the plan of salvation. Devotion to her, acknowledgment of her preeminence among all the saints, is not some Mediterranean aberration, nor the excess of the uninstructed; rather, it is the solid teaching of the magisterium of the Church. That Vatican II, animated as it was by ecumenical hopes, should have insisted on the role of Mary makes it clear that Mary is the means, not the obstacle, to Christian unity.

The Second Extraordinary Synod, which John Paul II called at the end of 1985 to assess the twenty years since the close of Vatican II and to revitalize the doctrine and goals of the Council, was equally insistent on Mary as "Mother of the Church."

It is well to recall this now, as we turn to consider some of the apparitions which have characterized the Marian age in which we live.

I said earlier that it would have been possible to make the points of this part of my little book with reference to Mary alone. Pilgrimages to her shrines, the cherishing of reminders of her saintly life, have been common practice over the centuries. There was a literary genre in medieval times devoted to the miracles of Mary.

Pierre Kunstmann has recently published a collection of medieval French narratives of Marian miracles, *Vierge et Merveille, Les miracles de Notre-Dame, narratifs du Moyen Age* (Paris, 1981). This work includes thirteen accounts, beginning with that of a pilgrim to Santiago de Compostela to whom the devil appears in the form of St. James and induces him to kill himself. As the devils are carrying away his soul, they run into St. James who is indignant that he has been impersonated. The Blessed Mother is invoked and through her intercession the soul is allowed to return to the body and work out its salvation. The details of the story are earthier than I have indicated.

There are some two thousand such stories in Latin;

in old French there are nearly five hundred in verse and six hundred in prose; and they are found as well in Anglo-Norman, English, German, and Norse. The best known Spanish collection is that of Gonzalo de Berceo, *Milagros de Nuestra Señora*, of which there is a good recent edition by Daniel Devoto, published in Madrid in 1985.

Of interest from a literary and historical point of view, such poems and stories attest to the common belief in Mary as chief interceder with her Son. The power of her requests is taken to be such that they are all but certain to be answered by God.

The Blessed Mother has appeared to saintly persons throughout the centuries, but since 1830 there has been a dramatic increase in the number of apparitions. Even as I write this, there are claims of many apparitions going on simultaneously — in Yugoslavia and Argentina, for example. There are some such claims that seem manifestly false and it is the healthy flip side of Marian devotion to be able to have a little fun at the expense of those who pretend to have had a vision. J.F. Powers once wrote a short story in which a woman claimed to have been visited by the Blessed Virgin and given a terribly important message which she was, however, reluctant to divulge. Finally, she is induced to speak. The message? Keep Minnesota green! Claims to private revelations should always be treated with caution. But there are many which have received approbation. Few would question that we are on safe ground in accepting Lourdes and

Fátima. Most of us would add others as well. But no one would think that such private revelations are part of the deposit of faith, as if one were bound to accept them.

One of the marks of the apparitions that have received the personal approval of bishops and popes is that they underline received doctrine and do not claim to add to it. Furthermore, there is an insistence on submission to the Church hierarchy. Fátima is noteworthy for the concern the Blessed Mother showed for the pope. But before looking at the great Marian apparitions of the past one hundred fifty years, mention should be made of Our Lady of Guadalupe.

OUR LADY OF GUADALUPE — The conversion of the Indians in Mexico can safely be attributed to our Lady's appearance to a fifty-seven-year-old Aztec convert on December 9, 1531. The Indian's name was Juan Diego. On his way to Mass, he heard birds singing unseasonally and, upon investigating, there stood before him a young girl, Aztec in appearance, who, as it turned out, was the Blessed Virgin Mary. She told Juan Diego to go to the local bishop and tell him that the Virgin Mother of God wished a church built right where she was standing in order that the Virgin might show her compassion to Juan Diego's people and to all others who would sincerely ask her help in their work and sorrows.

Juan Diego went off to the bishop, who listened to him and told him to come another time. He immediately returned to the site of the apparition and Mary told him to go back and repeat the message the following day. The bishop may have been less than happy to see him again so soon, but he asked the Indian to ask the lady for a sign. He returned and Mary told him to come back the following morning.

The next day, Juan Diego's uncle, with whom he lived, fell ill and he nursed him, missing his appointment with Mary. The uncle, on the verge of death, asked for the last sacraments and off Juan Diego went for the priest, going around the mountain on the opposite side so he wouldn't run into the Blessed Virgin. But she intercepted him. She assured him his uncle was cured and sent him to cut some flowers — in December! He found beautiful roses, filled his cape with them, and brought them to the Blessed Virgin. She rearranged them and said that the flowers were the sign the bishop wanted.

Off to the bishop he went, with the roses concealed in his tunic, emitting a fragrant odor. When he opened his tunic for the bishop, the roses fell out and the bishop fell to his knees. On the fabric of Juan Diego's cloak was the image of the Blessed Virgin as she had appeared to him. The bishop hung the cloak in his chapel, and Juan Diego went home to his uncle accompanied by friars and hidalgos, the latter being members of the Spanish lower nobility. The old man was in good health and he himself had received a visit from the Virgin who said she was Santa María de Guadalupe. Or so the Spaniards took him to say. It is now thought that the uncle was speaking Aztec, not broken Spanish, and what he said was, "Holy Mary of the stone serpent trodden upon" — meaning she had conquered their terrible god to whom so many human sacrifices had been made.

From 1532 to 1538, eight million Aztecs became Catholics. The church the Virgin requested was built and her image on Juan Diego's cape was exhibited there. Eventually a great basilica rose on the site and in it can still be seen, preserved miraculously, the Aztec's cape with the image of the Virgin on it in undiminished brilliance. This site is the object of pilgrimage, and many miracles have been wrought there. To this day, pilgrims stream to this shrine outside Mexico City where the Blessed Virgin first appeared in North America.

MARY OF THE MIRACULOUS MEDAL — Earlier I mentioned that the uncorrupted body of St. Catherine Labouré can be seen beneath the altar of the Blessed Virgin in a chapel on the Rue du Bac in Paris. Catherine was visited by the Blessed Virgin on several occasions and on one of them Mary described a medal she wanted distributed, a medal that has come to be called the Miraculous Medal.

Catherine joined the Daughters of Charity and lived in their convent on the Rue du Bac. She often had visions of St. Vincent de Paul whose heart is kept in a reliquary in the chapel there. It was on the eve of the feast of St. Vincent, July 18, 1830, that Catherine was awakened and led to the chapel by a child of about five years old, whom she took to be her guardian angel. The Blessed Virgin awaited her in the chapel. Our Lady sat down in a chair reserved for the director of the nuns; Catherine knelt before her and rested her hands on Mary's knees. "Come to the foot of this altar. There graces will be showered on you and on all who shall ask for them, rich and poor." These words of Mary are now inscribed over that altar.

On November 27, 1830, Catherine had another vision while praying in the chapel. She looked up and there was Mary in the sanctuary near a picture of St. Joseph. Mary held a globe near her heart and when that disappeared, rays of light streamed from her ringed fingers. An oval frame formed about her on which appeared the words: "O Mary, conceived without sin, pray for us who have recourse to thee." Catherine was told to have a medal struck which would represent Mary as she appeared. "Persons who wear it indulgenced will receive great graces, especially if they wear it around the neck: graces will be bestowed abundantly on those who have confidence." Mary turned and there appeared the reverse of the medal as it was eventually struck. It is doubtful that there are many Catholics who have not seen that medal and at least at one time worn it. It is easily the most common medal representing Mary.

That Catherine was the one to whom Mary had appeared was not known to other members of the order until she was on her deathbed. They knew only that one of their number had seen Mary. Catherine died on December 31, 1876.

Her body was buried in a crypt and was exhumed on March 21, 1933, following a procedure not unlike that described above for St. Bernadette. The outer wooden coffin had all but disintegrated, while the inner coffin of lead was preserved. That was cut away and an inner coffin of wood opened. Here are the words of an eyewitness: "The hands had slipped toward the side, but were white and natural looking. The cord of the rosary had decayed and the beads were loose in the coffin. The skin of the face had the appearance of parchment, but was entire. The eyes and mouth were closed."

Our interest now is on the apparition and its message. The message, as in the case of Our Lady of Guadalupe, is that the Blessed Mother will help those who appeal to her intercession. The crowds that come daily to the chapel on the Rue du Bac, the millions who wear the Miraculous Medal, can attest to the efficacy of her prayers. It is the confirmation of the doctrine that she was conceived free of original sin that is noteworthy about this apparition.

OUR LADY OF LOURDES — Although Mary appeared in 1846 at La Salette, a vision which had a tremendous impact on many, not least the famous author Leon Bloy, we will turn next to our Lady's appearance to Bernadette Soubirous at Lourdes. We have met Bernadette already in these pages, but far from her home at the convent where she lived until her death at the age of thirty-five.

The Blessed Virgin appeared to the poor and all but illiterate Bernadette in 1858 in the foothills of the Pyrenees in southern France and spoke to her in the language of the region which strikes one as a kind of mixture of French and Spanish.

Bernadette was out gathering firewood with her sister and another girl, a cousin, but had separated from them when the Blessed Mother appeared to her in the grotto of Massabielle, gesturing her to draw closer. Instinctively, Bernadette took out her beads and began to pray the rosary. Mary passed her own beads through her fingers as Bernadette prayed and joined her in the Glory be to the Father, at the end of the decades. The rosary being finished, the lady disappeared.

When Bernadette's mother heard what had happened at the grotto of Massabielle, she assured Bernadette it was nothing but an illusion, a figment of her imagination. Bernadette could not believe that. Here is the description she was to give of the lady she had seen. "She has the appearance of a young girl of sixteen or seventeen. She is dressed in a white robe, girdled at the waist with a blue ribbon which flows down all around it. A yoke closes it in graceful pleats at the base of the neck; the sleeves are long and tight-fitting. She wears upon her head a veil which is also white; this veil gives just a glimpse of her hair and then falls down at the back below her waist. Her feet are bare but covered by the last folds of her robe except at the point where a yellow rose shines upon each of them. She holds on her right arm a rosary of white beads with a chain of gold shining like the two roses on her feet."

Her mother did not want her to return to the grotto, indeed forbade her to do so, but some days later allowed the three girls to go back. They were joined by others along the way, perhaps told by Bernadette's sister what had happened before. Bernadette arrived there first, fell on her knees, and cried, "There she is." The others saw nothing, save the transformation in Bernadette and felt a change in the atmosphere of the place.

Not too long after that, the young girl saw our Lady again at the grotto. Instructed to return every day for fifteen days, Bernadette did, with difficulties, with larger and larger crowds accompanying her. She was told the lady wanted a chapel built here and that she should tell the curé. He answered that he had no money for a chapel. And he wanted Bernadette to ask the lady to identify herself. The answer when it came was this: *Que soy era Immaculada Councepciou* (I am the Immaculate Conception). Bernadette did not know what that meant. The doctrine had been proclaimed by the Holy Father only four years earlier.

The message of Lourdes is prayer and penance. Pray for poor sinners. Do penance. Mary will intercede for us. That Mary appeared to this simple peasant girl is doubtless part of the message. Bernadette herself, in her photographs, in what we are told of her at the time of the apparitions and later when she had become a nun at Nevers, comes through as a fascinating person, down to earth, unexcited, a little wary.

Mary's description of herself as the Immaculate Conception, as on the Miraculous Medal she instructed Catherine Labouré to have made, underscores the importance of that dogma.

The healing and cures, physical and spiritual, that have characterized Lourdes for over a century have made it part of the popular consciousness. Novelists from Franz Werfel to Irving Wallace have been attracted to these events and based works of fiction on them. *The Song of Bernadette* as a movie has influenced many.

In February of 1986, on the anniversary days of several of the apparitions, I was in Lourdes. It was cold and rainy, clearly the off season. I thought: You could shoot a cannon through these streets and not hit a pilgrim. I had arrived in the evening and, after renting a room, walked in a light drizzle down the streets between shuttered shops, crossed the river, and approached the great church that has been built over the grotto. It was eerie walking alone there. At the grotto itself were several others. I said my prayers and went back to my room.

In the morning I attended Mass in the rain at the grotto, getting under the overhang of the rock to keep the rain off my thinning hair. There was a goodly number there despite the weather. I thought of the replica of this grotto at Nevers. I thought of that other replica of Lourdes at the University of Notre Dame. The sense that one was in a holy place was strong.

"Do penance. Pray for sinners." That message continues to be heard. In season and out, the pilgrims come, asking Mary's intercession with her Son.

OUR LADY OF FÁTIMA — There was a new urgency in Mary's message to the three little shepherds of Fátima in 1917.

Before our Lady appeared to Lucia dos Santos (or Abóbora) and her cousins Francisco and Jacinta Marto, an angel appeared to them in 1916 when they were aged nine, eight, and six respectively. Already, the previous year, the three had seen a statuelike figure, almost transparent in the sun, that appeared above the trees when they were reciting the rosary. In the spring of 1916, out watching their flocks, the children took refuge from the rain, ate their lunch and said the rosary when there was a rushing of wind and they saw again the figure they had seen the year before. It drew closer and Lucy later wrote that it resembled a young man, about fourteen or fifteen years old, whiter than snow, transparent as crystal.

"Do not be afraid!" the heavenly apparition told the young shepherds. "I am the angel of peace. Pray with me."

They knelt and the angel taught them this prayer: "My God, I believe, I adore, I hope in, and I love you. I ask pardon for those who do not believe, do not adore, do not hope in, and do not love you."

The words etched themselves in the children's minds and they said the prayer over and over. But on another occasion, the angel appeared and wanted to know why they weren't praying. They were also to make sacrifices. How?

"Make of everything you can a sacrifice, and offer it to God as an act of reparation for the sins by which he is offended, and in supplication for the conversion of sinners. You will thus draw down peace upon your country. I am its Angel Guardian, the Angel of Portugal. Above all, accept and bear with submission the suffering which the Lord will send you."

As after the first apparition of the angel, the children felt taken out of themselves and immersed in a supernatural atmosphere. Yet a third time did the angel appear to them while they were reciting the prayer he had taught them before. He appeared in a great light, holding a chalice in his left hand with the Host suspended above it, from which drops of blood fell into the chalice. He left the chalice and Host suspended in air, knelt beside the children, and said the following prayer three times:

"Most Holy Trinity, Father, Son and Holy Spirit, I offer you the most precious body, blood, soul, and divinity of Jesus Christ, present in all the tabernacles of the world, in reparation for the outrages, sacrileges, and indifference with which he himself is offended, and through the infinite merits of his Sacred Heart and the Immaculate Heart of Mary, I beg of you the conversion of poor sinners."

The place of this apparition of the angel is found by angling off the Via Crucis at Fátima. Suddenly one comes upon a large sculpture of the angel appearing to the three children. It is set among the shrubs and trees in a most effective way.

Troubles at home gave Lucia an opportunity to know what it meant to offer things up in reparation for sins. As became apparent, these angelic visitations prepared the children for the remarkable events to come.

On May 13, 1917, the Blessed Virgin Mary appeared to them, telling them not to be afraid. When Lucia asks where she is from, our Lady replies, "I am from heaven." To Lucia's question "What does the Lady wish?" the Blessed Mother answers, "I have come to ask you to come here on six consecutive months on the thirteenth day at this same hour. After that I will tell you who I am and what I wish. I will come here a seventh time."

Lucia asks whether she will go to heaven. "Yes" is the reply. And Jacinta? "She too." And Francisco? "Yes, but he must pray many rosaries." They want to know the eternal fate of people who have recently died, and then the lady asks: "Are you willing to offer yourselves to God to bear all the sufferings he wills to send you, as an act of reparation for the sins by which he is offended, and of supplication for the conversion of sinners?"

Lucia says they are and the lady continues, "Then you are going to have much to suffer, but the grace of God will be your comfort." She opens her hands and light flows from them, seeming to penetrate into the innermost depths of the breasts and hearts of the children and it is as if they see themselves in God. Spontaneously they recite the prayer to the Trinity the angel had taught them, after which Mary tells them to pray the rosary every day for peace in the world and the end of the war.

In the second apparition, Lucia is told she must learn to read, since she will be left on earth while Jacinta and Francisco were soon to go to heaven. (The little brother and sister did indeed die young and, even as I write this,

Lucia, long a Carmelite nun, is still alive, in her late seventies.) Again light flows from the lady's hands and the three children feel submerged in God. Mary also shows them her Immaculate Heart.

The following month, on July 13, the third apparition took place, and now crowds come with the children. They are to say the rosary every day in honor of Our Lady of the Rosary, for she alone can bring peace to the world and put an end to the war. Lucia tells her that people want a miracle and is told to keep coming every month and in October the lady will reveal who she is and perform a miracle that all can see in order to believe. Then she teaches them a prayer to say when trouble comes: "Oh, Jesus, it is for love of you, for the conversion of sinners and in reparation for the sins committed against the Immaculate Heart of Mary."

On this occasion she gives the children a vision of hell where the damned writhe in the flames and the demons appear in horrible forms. She tells them that it is to save sinners from this fate that God wishes to establish devotion to her Immaculate Heart. If the children do what she asks, many souls will be saved, peace will come, the war will end. But, she adds, in the reign of Pius XI will come a worse war if men do not stop offending God. (Some may insist that World War II started during the pontificate of Pius XII, when Hitler attacked Poland on September 1, 1939; others will say the Second World War began in the reign of Pius XI, when Japan invaded Manchuria in 1931. But even if we disregarded the Manchurian invasion, we cannot deny that events leading up to World War II took place while Pius XI was pope.) To go on with our story, Mary tells the shepherd children she wants the Holy Father to consecrate Russia to her Immaculate Heart in order to prevent that war. And there is more that Lucia is to keep secret.

It is on this occasion that Mary asks that at the end of each decade of the rosary, after the Glory be to the Father, this prayer be added: "My Jesus, forgive us, deliver us from the fire of hell, draw all souls to heaven, especially those in greatest need."

Lucia has written down an account of each of the apparitions. The recurrent note is prayer and sacrifice in reparation for sin, with not only the eternal fate of sinners hanging in the balance but also the future of the globe. War is a punishment for sin; peace will be the reward for repentance and sacrifice.

And then Saturday, October 13, arrives, the day when a great miracle will give proof of what the children have seen. Mary asks that a chapel in her honor, to be called Our Lady of the Rosary, be built in the Cova da Iria, and that the rosary be recited every day. The rain had been falling steadily, but now it stopped and then the crowd all saw the sun rotate in the sky, spin like a cartwheel, and then come hurtling toward earth, terrifying them all. Meanwhile the children were shown a series of visions of the Holy Family, then our Lady and our Lord together. And then it was over.

The story of Fátima did not end with the apparitions

of 1917. Lucia became a nun and experienced further apparitions in 1925, 1926, and 1929. Mary requested that the Holy Father consecrate Russia to her Immaculate Heart in order to prevent the spread of Russia's errors through the world. Concern for Russia had been expressed already in the apparition of July 13, 1917, in remarks the visionaries were instructed to keep secret. The "secret of Fátima," as it has come to be called, has not yet been fully divulged. Lucia wrote it down for her bishop and eventually it was sent to Rome and the understanding was that it would be made known by the pope in 1960. That did not happen. Here is the chronology of the secret.

Lucia wrote it out on December 25, 1943 and January 9, 1944. She put the text in an envelope, sealed it, and gave it to the bishop of Leira on June 17, 1944. The bishop enclosed it in a larger envelope, dated December 8, 1945, with the instruction that it be handed to the cardinal-patriarch of Lisbon after the bishop's death. In March of 1957 the envelope was turned over to the apostolic nuncio in Lisbon. Pius XII decided not to read the text. It was put into the hands of John XXIII, who read it in the presence of Cardinal Ottaviani and others on May 13, 1960. The pope decided against making any announcement, saying, "It does not concern the years of my pontificate." Paul VI presumably read it and it is supposed that this influenced his decision to visit Fátima. Pope John Paul II has also visited Fátima. Cardinal Ratzinger, in the recently published *Report on the Faith*, gave an affirmative reply to the question whether he had read the secret of Fátima. Why has it not been made public? The cardinal said that it would be thought sensational if it became known.

Let us be clear what is meant by the secret of Fátima. It concerns what the three children were told on July 13, 1917. This is how Lucia described that day.

A few moments after arriving at the Cova da Iria, near the holm oak, where a large number of people were praying the rosary, we saw the flash of light once more, and a moment later our Lady appeared on the holm oak.

"What do you want of me?" I asked.

"I want you to come here on the thirteenth of next month, to continue to pray the rosary every day in honor of Our Lady of the Rosary, in order to obtain peace for the world and the end of the war, because only she can help you."

"I would like to ask you to tell us who you are, and to work a miracle so that everybody will believe that you are appearing to us."

"Continue to come here every month. In October, I will tell you who I am and what I want, and I will perform a miracle for all to see and believe."

I then made some requests, but I cannot recall just what they were. What I do remember is that our Lady said it was necessary for such people to pray the rosary in order to obtain these graces during the year. And she continued:

"Sacrifice yourselves for sinners, and say many

times, especially whenever you make some sacrifice: O Jesus, it is for love of you, for the conversion of sinners, and in reparation for the sins committed against the Immaculate Heart of Mary.''

As our Lady spoke these last words, she opened her hands once more, as she had done during the two previous months. The rays of light seemed to penetrate the earth, and we saw as it were a sea of fire. Plunged into this fire were demons and souls in human form, like transparent burning embers, all blackened or burnished bronze, floating about in the conflagration, now raised into the air by the flames that issued from within themselves together with great clouds of smoke, now falling back on every side like sparks in huge fires, without weight or equilibrium, amid shrieks and groans of pain and despair, which horrified us and made us tremble with fear. (It must have been this sight which caused me to cry out, as people say they heard me.) The demons could be distinguished by their terrifying and repellent likeness to frightful and unknown animals, black and transparent like burning coals. Terrified and as if to plead for succor, we looked up at our Lady, who said to us so kindly and so sadly:

"You have seen hell where the souls of poor sinners go. To save them, God wishes to establish in the world devotion to my Immaculate Heart. If what I say to you is done, many souls will be saved and there will be peace. The war is going to end; but

if people do not cease offending God, a worse one
will break out during the pontificate of Pius XI.
When you see a night illumined by an unknown light,
know that this is the great sign given you by God
that he is about to punish the world for its crimes,
by means of war, famine, and persecutions of the
Church and of the Holy Father.

"To prevent this, I shall come to ask for the
consecration of Russia to my Immaculate Heart,
and the Communion of Reparation on the First Saturdays. If my requests are heeded, Russia will be
converted and there will be peace; if not, she will
spread her errors throughout the world, causing
wars and persecutions of the Church. The good will
be martyred, the Holy Father will have much to suffer, various nations will be annihilated. In the end,
my Immaculate Heart will triumph. The Holy Father will consecrate Russia to me, and she will be
converted, and a period of peace will be granted to
the world. In Portugal, the dogma of the faith will
always be preserved. . . ." [From this point on, our
Lady told the children things that they were to keep
secret; they of course could tell Francisco who, it
should be noted, could not hear the Blessed Mother
during the apparitions.]

Now, at the end of this account, after the remark
about Portugal, is where the as yet unrevealed portion of
the secret begins. That is what the popes have chosen not
to make public because, as Cardinal Ratzinger has ex-

plained, it would be judged sensational if made public.

Given the disarray in the Church, the defections from the priesthood and from the religious life, the dissent among theologians that has misled so many about the dogmatic and moral teaching of the Church, given the attempt on the life of the Holy Father himself, it is hard to know what else lies in store that could be considered sensational. From the vantage point of Fátima, there is little doubt that Marxism and the Soviet Union are the scourge God is using to punish us for our sins. But the message of Fátima is primarily one of hope. It tells us what must be done if sinners are to be saved from hell and a period of peace granted the world. There must be sacrifice, reparation for sin, and there must be devotion to the Immaculate Heart of Mary. And one of the ways of accomplishing this is to go to Mass and receive Holy Communion on the first Saturdays of five consecutive months, confess one's sins, and pray for the Holy Father.

With respect to the still-undisclosed secret of Fátima, those who have studied the matter closely — for example, Joaquin María Alonso, *La Verdad Sobre El Secreto de Fátima* (1976) — have drawn a number of conclusions. First, it does not contain predictions of catastrophic political and/or military events. Second, it concerns consequences within the Church if devotion to the Immaculate Heart of Mary is not practiced and Russia is not consecrated to her by the pope together with all the bishops. Third, the message is specifically for the Holy Father. The portion of Lucia's account of the apparition of July 13, 1917 that begins the still undivulged secret reads: "In Portugal, the dogma of the faith will always be preserved. . . ." It has seemed reasonable to conclude that the message goes on to speak of the loss of the Catholic faith in many lands.

MORE RECENT APPARITIONS — We have not mentioned Mary's apparitions at Knock, Ireland, in 1879, nor those at Beauraing, Belgium, in 1932-1933, and in Banneux, also in Belgium, in 1933. If one had to select a single reason for all these apparitions it would be maternal warning, maternal concern, maternal reminding of what is demanded of us as Christians. Apparitions are a powerful underscoring of what we already know, making vivid to us the love Mary bears us and the role she is meant to play in the Church. The message, in a word, is *Repent!* That Mary indicates what will happen if people do not stop offending God, that some of these revelations have never been made public, should not overwhelm our curiosity so that we lose sight of the salutary warnings.

That the great graces of Lourdes and Fátima and the other apparitions have not had the desired effect seems clear from the fact that almost daily there are reports of new apparitions. Obviously, it would be frivolous to go dashing off to check out every such report. But some gather momentum and force themselves on us, so to speak. In Argentina, for example, it would be hard not to become aware of the reported apparitions at San Nicolas which began on September 25, 1983 and continue to the present.

Not long ago I had a Fulbright Fellowship to Argentina, heard about San Nicolas, and visited the shrine on September 25, 1985, the second anniversary of the beginning of the alleged revelations. San Nicolas, a beautiful little town, is on the Paraná River, nearly four hours by train from Buenos Aires. In the cathedral, there is a statue of Our Lady of the Rosary, blessed by Pope Leo XIII in 1884. It is when kneeling before this statue that a woman (whose name is not made known) receives messages from Mary. These are frequent, almost daily, and those through July of 1985 have been published in *Mensajes*. A feature of these brief messages is that they usually include passages of Scripture. But the message is familiar: we must consecrate ourselves to the Immaculate Heart of Mary; we must pray, especially the rosary; we must read and ponder the Scriptures; these are terrible times and we must offer sacrifices for others; we must do penance; we must beware of the evil one; we must be loyal to the Church and its pastors; we must go to confession and receive Holy Communion frequently.

The cathedral was jammed the day I was there, the sanctuary full of priests concelebrating Mass. In a side aisle, the faithful moved slowly toward the front to honor the Virgin, represented by a statue. From the cathedral it is but a short walk to the site where Mary wants a shrine built. There were swarms of people here too, with the rosary being recited constantly. After joining in, I walked across the field to where I could get a look at the river which at this spot is broken into dozens of channels.

The Paraná. In North America the name of this river brings to mind the piranha, the fish whose "killer" reputation has spawned many a horror story. The river itself looked indolent and peaceful. But I didn't go for a swim.

And Medjugorje! The daily apparitions that have been taking place in this Yugoslav town, involving at the outset six children, have received worldwide attention, as much for what may seem to us to be their unlikely setting — in a Communist country — but also because of ecclesiastical quarrels concerning the parish in which the events occur.

The apparitions began outside in June of 1981, but when people were forbidden to congregate at the place, Mary began to appear to the children in the village church. Evidently she appears to them daily still. Despite the frequency of the appearances there is not a vast amount of sayings of the Virgin. Indeed, the children rely on memory and do not seem to feel obliged to remember everything. They have been given secrets, however, but the message seems the same as Fátima: "I am the Queen of Peace. There are serious tensions in the world and if things go on as they are the result will be bad. Salvation is to be found in peace alone, but to have peace there must be a return to God."

If the message is the same, it is more urgent. Prayer and fasting are stressed. Two days a week the children take only bread and water, and they frequent the sacraments. Here are some of the messages the children claim the Blessed Mother has given them:

• Many Christians have lost their faith because they did not pray. With prayer and fasting it is possible to prevent even war.

• I particularly recommend that you go to daily Mass.

• You must believe that Satan exists. God is permitting him to test the Church, but not to destroy it. When the secrets committed to you have been realized, the power of Satan will be destroyed. He has become aggressive now: he destroys marriages, stirs up quarrels between priests, bedevils people . . . so protect yourselves from him with prayer, with fasting; above all with community prayer. Carry with you in your wallet holy objects, renew the use of holy water. Satan can do nothing against one who has firm faith in God.

• Don't seek after strange things. Everything is in the Gospels.

Signs and wonders? The children were told they would have many of them, culminating in a final miracle that will be seen by everyone and will be directed particularly to atheists. Books on the apparitions speak of a repetition of the solar miracle of Fátima at Medjugorje on August 2, 1981, and of other strange phenomena in the heavens.

The Church exercises great caution in the matter of apparitions, and both San Nicolas and Medjugorje are far from being endorsed or approved. The books on Medjugorje I have seen are all careful to discuss both pros and cons of authenticity. But its message, being basically evangelical, is hardly controversial.

There is one particularly interesting statement attributed to the Blessed Virgin by the children at Medjugorje. This apparition, she told them, will be the last.

Let me end this account of the miracles of Mary and her shrines with some remarks about "La Madonna del Miracolo" in the Basilica S. Andrea delle Fratte in Rome, and permit me a slightly personal note.

When I was in Rome to follow the Second Extraordinary Synod, which ran for two weeks beginning in late November and culminating on the Feast of the Immaculate Conception, December 8, 1985, I stayed in the Hotel di Malta, its name grander than the reality, near the Spanish Steps. In the next block there was, I knew, the house in which Bernini had lived and just catty-corner from it a church I had never been in. My wife and I had noticed it many times, usually seeing it from behind, being fascinated by its tower, and going on. During my Extraordinary Synod visit, I decided to go around to that church for Mass.

The church, as I soon discovered, was called the Basilica S. Andrea delle Fratte. In it were some massive statues of angels by Bernini. But the attraction of the church, its devotional center, was a side altar where the daily Masses are said. A beautiful painting of Mary as she appears on the Miraculous Medal hangs over the altar, and two white marble busts flank the alcove in which the altar stands. The Masses were well attended and on some days went on at half-hour intervals or less. Of course I wondered what it all meant. There are so

many special places in Rome that one can become jaded.
I do not say I was blasé, but I had no idea what a treasure
I had stumbled on.

The initial event was the conversion of January 21,
1842, of a Jewish businessman from Strasbourg named
Alphonse Ratisbonne. Engaged to marry, on a long trip
so that he might return to a fiancée closer to mar-
riageable age, he stopped in Rome, not intending to, and
stayed on. He met a man who dared him to recite the
Memorare and wear a Miraculous Medal, and
Ratisbonne, who claimed he hated the Church, did both.
And then one fateful day he entered the Basilica S. Andrea delle Fratte, Mary appeared to him, and he was converted on the spot. He became a priest and eventually
went to Jerusalem where he worked for the conversion of
the Jews. He died in the Holy Land in 1884.

The chapel and the painting of Mary commemorate
his conversion, and one of the busts flanking the alcove is
of Ratisbonne. One of the popes called this chapel the
Lourdes of Rome; it is a favored place of pilgrimage, the
walls covered with plaques acknowledging favors. The
marble bust across from Ratisbonne's is of St. Max-
ımilian Kolbe, who celebrated his first Mass at that side
altar. It was here that Thérèse Martin is said to have
come during that famous visit to Rome before she entered the Carmel of Lisieux. And it was here that Mother
Teresa of Calcutta came on Saturday evening, December
7, 1985. She was in Rome as a special participant in the
Extraordinary Synod and she had come to the Basilica

S. Andrea delle Fratte to honor the Blessed Virgin, and also to talk to the parishioners. As soon as she entered the church, there was an almost palpable alteration of the atmosphere. The Synod Fathers had said that what the Church needs most is saints. Hasn't that been the message of Mary in her various apparitions? Isn't that the point of all the shrines and statues and pictures, reminders everywhere of the Mother of God, and of her unique role in the work of salvation?

Miracles catch the eye, there is little doubt of that. But they are meant to draw it on to the source of the miracle.

In that basilica in Rome, to which she had come as a pilgrim, Mother Teresa spoke of what is going wrong with the world and what we must do. She conveyed a vivid sense of the communion of the saints, of the transcendent importance of human life, of God's love. She spoke with a directness that moved us all deeply.

PART THREE

The Theology
of Miracles

Prologue

The preceding parts of this little book have put before us a great deal of material and food for thought.

Holy Scripture, it is clear, is replete with miracles, both in the Old Testament and in the New. Since the Bible is not just a happenstance collection of old texts, but the revealed word of God, on the authenticity of whose canonical books we have the assurance of the Church, the Bible must be viewed as a whole, however diverse its parts.

For this reason the Old Testament and the signs and wonders recorded in its pages point ahead by way of figures to the Messiah, to God incarnate, to Jesus Christ. This is clear from the way in which Jesus refers to himself as the fulfillment of scriptural prophecies, as the referent of earlier events, but also in the preaching of the

Apostles. After Pentecost, the Apostles are particularly concerned to show their fellow Jews that Jesus is the Messiah for whom they had been waiting.

The prophets had worked miracles, but Jesus works them in his own name, showing not only that he is from God, but that he *is* God. After Christ, the Apostles work miracles to provide signs of the truth of what they are saying.

Miracles, then, are — in a manner of speaking — an ordinary element in Judeo-Christian religious belief. Although I have glancingly indicated some reasons for them and what their function is, the reality of miracles raises a host of questions on which the believer will want to reflect.

Those who engage in such reflection as a profession, performing a very special role among the people of God, are called theologians. Theological doctrines and explanations have, generally speaking, the authority of the arguments or of the fruitfulness of the explication advanced. Theological conclusions and doctrines are not to be confused with the official teaching Church, what has come to be called the magisterium. It is the Holy Father and the bishops of the world in union with the pope, who speak with the authority of their office, and can speak infallibly, as to the content of the deposit of faith. But whether speaking infallibly as the extraordinary magisterium or only as the ordinary magisterium, pope and bishops always command the respectful assent of the faithful.

Of course when the theologian draws our attention to what has been infallibly defined, that portion of what he says commands unquestioned assent. And the starting points of theological reflection will always be of that kind — either defined doctrine or what has been revealed by Scripture. Furthermore, when theological reflection over the centuries arrives at a consensus on various matters, that will carry weight with the believer. The Fathers and Doctors of the Church have their own special authority, needless to say, and in theological matters the authority of St. Thomas Aquinas is paramount.

In this third part, I want to address the questions that arise from the fact of miracles, not so much by engaging in theological reflection myself, but rather as relating to the reader the thoughts of theologians. As it happens, the question of miracles has also received a good deal of philosophical attention, so I can hazard, in my capacity as philosopher, a thought or two *in propria persona* on the less exalted level of philosophy.

These are the issues we shall consider now in the third and final part of this book:

✓ The Magisterium and Miracles.
✓ Theological Tradition on Miracles.
✓ St. Thomas Aquinas on Miracles.
✓ The Possibility of Miracles.
✓ Can Miracles Be Seen?
✓ Between Skepticism and Credulity.

CHAPTER SEVEN

The Magisterium and Miracles

One of the great documents of Vatican I is the dogmatic constitution *Dei Filius* on the Catholic faith. Its chapters deal with God the Creator of all things, revelation, faith, and faith and reason; these are followed by certain rules, or *canones*. Chapter 3, "On Faith," states that God provides external signs as arguments on behalf of revelation (Denzinger-Schönmetzer, No. 3009) and among the *canones* we find this carefully worded statement on miracles:

"If anyone should say that there can be no miracles, and that all accounts of them, even those contained in sacred Scripture, are to be thought of as fables or myths; or that miracles cannot be certainly known; or that they can never be rightly used to prove the divine origin of the

Christian religion: let him be anathema" (Denzinger-Schönmetzer, No. 3034).

Pope St. Pius X, in a motu proprio dated September 1, 1910, condemning Modernist errors, said this: "I admit and recognize as most certain signs of the divine origin of the Christian religion, as divine deeds, chiefly miracles and prophecies, and I hold them to be especially adapted to the understanding of all ages and of all men, including of the present time" (Denzinger-Schönmetzer, No. 3539).

The text from Vatican I stresses three things about miracles: (1) accounts of them, particularly biblical accounts, are not to be dismissed as fables or myths; (2) miracles can be known with certainty; and (3) miracles are a proof of the divine origin of Christianity.

St. Pius X stresses that (1) miracles prove the divine origin of Christianity and (2) they are not to be dismissed as fitting only to earlier times and to minds less advanced than our own.

From the Council of Ephesus (431), we can cite St. Cyril's Third Letter to Nestorius to the effect that Christ performed wonders to demonstrate his divinity (cf. *Conciliorum Oecumenicorum Decreta*, Bologna, 1973, p. 57.17-24). From the Council of Constantinople (553): "If anyone should say that the Word of God who performed miracles is other than Christ who suffered, or the Word of God other than Christ born of woman, and exists in him as one thing in another and not as one and the same Our Lord Jesus Christ, the Word of God incarnate and made man, both the miracles his as well as the sufferings he voluntarily accepted in the flesh: let such a one be anathema" (*Conciliorum*, p. 114.23-34). The Third Council of Constantinople (680-681) reiterated this (p. 129.20-25).

These statements underscore the truth that it is the same Lord Jesus Christ who performs miracles and who suffers — the miracles clearly being taken as a sign of Christ's divinity, and his passion as a sign of his humanity.

Vatican II, which speaks in a special way to our times, has several statements about miracles. For example, in *Lumen Gentium*, or the "Dogmatic Constitution on the Church," Christ's miracles are said to show "that the kingdom has already come on earth" (No. 5). And in the "Dogmatic Constitution on Divine Revelation" (again quoting from *Vatican Council II: The Conciliar and Post-Conciliar Documents*), we read, "As a result, he himself [that is, Jesus] — to see whom is to see the Father (cf. Jn. 14:9) — completed and perfected Revelation and comfirmed it with divine guarantees. He did this by the total fact of his presence and self-manifestation — by words and works, signs and miracles, but above all by his death and glorious resurrection from the dead, and finally by sending the Spirit of truth. He revealed that God was with us, to deliver us from the darkness of sin and death, and to raise us up to eternal life" (No. 4). In the "Declaration on Religious Liberty," we read that Jesus "supported and confirmed his preaching by miracles to arouse the faith of his hearers and give them assurance, but not to coerce them. He did indeed denounce the unbelief of his listeners but he left vengeance to God until the day of judgment" (No. 11).

The first two passages link miracles and signs of Christ's divinity and mission. The third adds to that the observation that this link is not coercive, but with the significant qualification that failure to recognize the link is not without fault.

Vatican II, again in *Lumen Gentium* (No. 58), talking of the role of Mary, stresses that it was through her intercession that the miracle at the wedding feast of Cana was performed.

The Third Epistle of Cyril to Nestorius also speaks of the miracles performed by the saints: "Finally this same spirit, working glorious miracles through the hands of the holy apostles as well, glorified Our Lord Jesus Christ after he ascended into heaven" (*Conciliorum*, p. 57.32-36).

The Council of Trent (1545-1563) tells us that "through God's saints miracles and salutary examples are put before our eyes that we might imitate the life and customs of the saints and be stirred up to love God and foster piety" (*Conciliorum*, p. 775.31-35); it also warns that "no new miracles are to be recognized nor new relics received without the bishop's knowledge and approval" (p. 776.10-12).

From such passages we can conclude that it is part of Catholic faith that Christ performed miracles, that the scriptural accounts must not be interpreted as tall stories, and that the Apostles and other saintly persons for various reasons are given the power to perform miracles.

What such passages do not give us, as such, is a definition of miracle. Let us accordingly turn to the theological tradition on miracles.

CHAPTER EIGHT

Theological Tradition on Miracles

Historians tell us that in the early centuries, the Fathers of the Church had things to say about miracles but did not provide a formal definition of miracle. The Gospel miracles are seen as proving the divinity of Christ. Origen considered miracles to be an external criterion of revelation and went on to distinguish miracles from wonderful deeds performed by magicians and others because of the purpose of miracles: the salvation of souls, the reform of morals, adoration of God. Some Fathers, like Arnobius, simply say that Christ performed a lot more miracles than worldly wonder-workers. Justin sees the divine origin of Christ's miracles in the fact that they fulfill prophecies. With Tertullian, this becomes an argument against the unbelief of Jews.

St. Augustine is said to be the first to attempt a definition of what a miracle is, but it turns out to be difficult to match all the things he says of miracles to his express definition. "I call a miracle any difficult or uncustomary thing which appears, exceeding the hope and expectation of the onlookers" (*De utilitate credendi*, xvi, 34). Augustine does not seem to require divine intervention for the appearance of the difficult and uncustomary thing. Indeed, any wonder or marvel — willed by God of course — can provoke men to tend to the truth. This puts miraculous events on the same footing as natural events, since natural events can fulfill the function Augustine assigns to miracles. After Augustine, authors tend to retain this fusion, stressing how marvelous creation and the natural world are, capable of exciting the mind and heart to faith and love of God. Nonetheless, in the medieval literature on miracles, there is the suggestion of a distinction between the miraculous event and a natural event.

St. Anselm of Canterbury distinguished three orders: that of nature, that of human action, and that of the divine will, the last being the realm of the miraculous. Emerging is the notion that the miracle is a direct intervention of God. The Scholastics work with Augustine's definition of course; Alexander of Hales, however, will point out that "uncustomary" in the definition does not mean simply that the event is rare, but that, even if it happens frequently, it does so against the accustomed course of nature. St. Albert the Great will say that although the event is beyond the expectation of the observer, this actually means beyond the expectation of nature, not merely beyond the expectation of grace.

I am following here the account given in the magnificent article on miracles in A. Michel's *Dictionnaire de la théologie catholique*. The account sees the theological tradition as gradually evolving and clarifying until with St. Thomas Aquinas full clarity is achieved.

CHAPTER NINE

St. Thomas Aquinas on Miracles

Like his predecessors, St. Thomas Aquinas takes his cue from St. Augustine and, in the *Summa Theologiae* (Ia.105.7), quotes the following definition of the bishop of Hippo, from *Contra Faustum*: "When God does things against the known and customary course of nature, they are called great or wonderful things." Let us look at the body of this article which asks: "Whether all the things God does outside the natural order of things are miracles?"

"I reply that the word *miracle* comes from wonder, but wonder arises when the result is manifest and the cause obscure, as one might wonder when he sees an eclipse of the sun, not knowing its cause, as Aristotle says at the outset of the *Metaphysics*. The cause of an effect can be known to some yet unknown to others, so something can be a wonder to one and not to another, as the eclipse is a wonder to the uninstructed but not to the astronomer. *Miracle* suggests something full of wonder, whose cause is unknown simply and absolutely. This cause is God. Hence what God does outside of causes known to us are called miracles.''

This is a typical Thomistic passage. It begins with the common or garden-variety sense of the word "wonder" — we can wonder at any event when we do not know what brought it about — but that is relative to the knowledge or ignorance of the observer. One man's wonder is another man's science. Beyond this state of affairs, Thomas continues, "miracle" suggests something wonderful through and through, such that no one grasps its cause. This condition is fulfilled when God is the cause of the event beyond the usual course of nature. Thomas uses "beyond" (*praeter*), not "against" (*contra*), known natural explanations.

Are the creation of the world and the justification of sinners miracles? They are beyond the natural order and only God can do them. No, Thomas says, these are not properly called miracles, precisely because they are not such that they can come about through other causes, so they cannot be said to be "beyond the order of nature" in the required sense. The implication here is that the miraculous effect may be one that could be produced by secondary causes, but then it would not be miraculous.

Thomas makes St. Albert's distinction between "the

hope of nature" and "the hope of grace" his own in gloss-ing the term "unexpected" in Augustine's first defini-tion.

What does beyond or above the natural order of things mean? "Something is said to be above the capaci-ty of nature, not only because of the nature of what is done, but also because of the way and order of doing it." This precision allows for the implication we noted in the passage quoted above.

What is implied throughout but is not stressed be-cause it is taken to be obvious is that the miraculous event must be observable, something seen.

What, then, is a miracle? Some imposing and unusual observable event which in the circumstances can only have been caused by God and whose purpose is to draw the mind beyond the natural to the supernatural.

Thomas's explanation of the three elements of Au-gustine's first definition of miracle — (1) uncustomary; (2) beyond the hope or capacity of nature; (3) difficult — can be summed up as follows:

1. *Uncustomary* — the miraculous event is an ex-ceptional event, outside the normal or common course of events. The "wonders of nature" would not then be won-ders or miracles in the required sense.

2. *Beyond the hope or capacity of nature* — the natural powers of the subject cannot explain the effect in question.

3. *Difficult* — the result surpasses all created pow-ers and can only be produced by God.

This summary is open to discussion on two grounds. First, does it accurately portray the thought of St. Thomas? Second, does it give us the concept of miracle effectively used by the Church?

On the first score, the summary takes insufficient account of Aquinas's threefold gloss on "beyond the capacity of nature" (*Summa Theologiae*, Ia.105.7.2m). The thing that happens may be meant, but the way and the order in which it happens can also be meant. This passage does not give us the restrictive view of the summary. There seems no need to overlook the fact that miraculous events involve natural causes. God's direct intervention need not mean a total absence of intermediate and secondary causes. The main thing is that the result is not one that would be produced by natural causes alone and in the ordinary course of events.

From the time of David Hume, skeptics have argued that the traditional conception of a miracle is simply incoherent, that it defines that which cannot happen and, since this is so, claims by people to have witnessed miracles must be dealt with as we usually deal with claims that the impossible is possible.

CHAPTER TEN

The Possibility of Miracles

It may seem that the concept of a miracle is impossible since if (a) the common course of nature is as God wills it, and (b) a miracle is an event which is outside of, even contrary to, the ordinary course of nature, it would seem to follow that (c) a miracle amounts to a thwarting of God's will.

This objection relies on too narrow a notion of God's will. As Cardinal Newman wrote, "The Miracles of Scripture, for instance, are irregularities in the economy of nature, but with a moral end; forming one instance out of many, of the providence of God, that is, an instance of occurrences in the natural world with a final cause. Thus, while they are exceptions to the laws of one system, they may coincide with those of another. They profess to be the evidence of a Revelation, the criterion of a divine message. To consider them as mere exceptions to physical order, is to take a very incomplete view of them. It is to degrade them from the station which they hold in the plans and provisions of the Divine Mind, and to strip them of their real use and dignity; for as naked and isolated facts they do but deform, an harmonious system" (*Essays on Miracles*, London, 1870, pp. 4-5). The details of this contrast are a bit puzzling, but the point seems clear. God's comprehensive purpose in creating — his providence — is achieved by the normal course of nature and by miraculous events. We expect Newman, of course, to lean heavily on miracles as evidence of the supernatural; it is to call men's attention to the supernatural that God performs, and enables others to perform, miracles.

Nonetheless, Newman's contrast — he was writing at the age of twenty-five — is reminiscent of St. Thomas's approach to the subject (*Summa Theologiae*, Ia.105.6). Any cause produces an order, an arrangement, in its effects, Thomas writes, and with the multiplication of causes there is a multiplication of orders, one being subordinate to another, as cause is subordinate to cause. Take an example from human affairs. On the head of the household depends the order within the domestic community, but that order is contained within the civil order which depends on the ruler of the city, and that in turn is contained within the order of the realm which depends upon the king.

Given that idea, if the order of things is considered as depending on the first cause, then God can do nothing against the order of things, since then he would obviously be working at cross-purposes, against himself. But if the order of things is considered insofar as it depends on a secondary cause, then God can do something outside the order of things. God is not subject to the order established by secondary causes; rather, that order is subject to him; the natural order does not proceed from God by a necessity of his nature, but voluntarily; consequently, he could bring about another order of things than that which de facto exists. Hence he can, when he wills, act outside the order that does exist, when he wishes — as, for example, by producing without secondary causes effects normally produced by secondary causes, or by producing effects beyond the capacity of secondary causes to produce.

In order to establish the theoretical impossibility of miracles, one would have to show that God, in creating the world, wills that he will never intervene in the natural world in order to produce variations from what would normally be produced by created causes. If that were the assumption of creation, then miracles would tell against God's immutability, and thus would be impossible in principle. But there seems little reason to accept this as a condition of creation.

We are far more likely today, in our view of the natural world, to find a place for random occurrences in it, so that the random itself is natural. This supplants the view that whatever occurs in the natural world happens with rigorous necessity. The miracle would then disrupt this necessary unfolding. But if one begins with the assumption that everything happens necessarily, simply issuing from its antecedents without any possibility of an alternative occurring, miracles have been defined out of the world along with the random.

A view of the natural world that accepts randomness is not just, as such, an acceptance of the miraculous, needless to say. But the notion of a created world which naturally includes necessary and regular and random occurrences seems conceptually more hospitable to the possibility of miracles than does a deterministic view of the natural world. A fully deterministic view must conclude that free choice is also impossible, so the hostility of such an outlook to Christianity is pretty thorough.

There still are those who, appealing to the progress of science, suggest that we know things today which render the idea of miraculous occurrences ridiculous. Of course this is not true. Arguments against the possibility of miracles are bad arguments. They rely not on science but on a misconception of what science enables us to know. Other arguments against miracles rely on false assumptions as to what creation entails with regard to God's causing events outside the regular course of the world he creates.

We must be very careful not to think of miracles as impossible events which nonetheless God brings about. Of course the events may be impossible from one point of view and not from another. If someone were to say that it is impossible for a man to go out to the cemetery and call out to a dead person and thereby raise him from the dead, who would say him nay? I can't raise the dead, and neither can you. No man can do it. We don't have that power. Nor could Jesus do it insofar as he is human. Jesus raised the son of the Widow of Nain and Lazarus from the dead because Jesus is divine as well as human. When Peter and Paul raised the dead to life, they did not do so on their own, but with the power of God that had been given to them on that occasion. What is impossible for mere man to do, is possible for God.

The miraculous event is one that is impossible from any point of view other than divine intervention. What happens might, in other circumstances, have come about as the result of natural causes or causes less than supernatural (that is, attributable to God), but in a particular set of circumstances the effect or event is not one that can be explained in the usual way. Someone who loses his sight may regain it in such a way that we would not speak of a miracle. An operation, an eye transplant, whatever, might restore sight. But when Jesus restores sight or grants sight to one born blind simply by willing that effect, we are in the presence of one whose powers exceed the natural, the human.

It can be said then that miraculous events are impossible to everyone but God or someone acting with a power granted to him by God. When it is asked whether miracles are possible, what is being asked is whether it is conceivable, coherent, or logically possible, that such special interventions of God are compatible with the natural order of things. Aquinas's conception of subordinate causes and subordinate orders enables him to formulate an affirmative answer to the question.

CHAPTER ELEVEN

Can Miracles Be Seen?

The question may not seem serious. If the miraculous event must be something visible, what sense can there be in asking if miracles can be seen?

I raise the question because it seems to be raised by scriptural accounts themselves. Christ performed miracles that were seen by many, but not everyone believed. Those who refused to believe, refused to take what they had seen as a sign of the divinity of Christ, as a divine endorsement of his message. The Pharisees suggested that Christ drove out devils by the power of Beelzebul, not by the power of God. But, if a miracle is defined as an event that can only be brought about by the intervention of God, such disbelief and refusal to accept are a denial that what was seen was caused by divine intervention.

Is such a denial logically inconsistent? It would be clearly incoherent for someone to say that he had witnessed X, which he agrees could only have come about by divine intervention but that he did not think it had come about by divine intervention. This would be like holding simultaneously that X is a miracle and that X is not a miracle.

Let us consider some other reactions to scriptural miracles so that we can get clearer on what it is like to, in some sense, witness a miracle and yet not accept that a miracle has occurred.

After our Lord's resurrection, the Jews assumed that the body of Jesus had been stolen. They even bribed the soldiers to spread that story lest the Apostles convince the people that Jesus had risen from the dead. Did the priests know and accept that Christ had risen from the dead and then deny it? If so, their denial would have to be treated as a lie. Or did they simply refuse to accept the testimony of those soldiers who had seen the empty tomb? Accepting that testimony would have had implications from which, presumably, they shrank. On the other hand, when the priests pondered how they might kill Lazarus so that people would stop talking about his resurrection, it seems clear that they were willfully refusing to accept the obvious implications of the event. Thus, it seems possible for the miracle to be accepted as a miracle — as something that cannot be explained save by the special intervention of God — and still refuse to accept the consequences of that recognition.

Many saw Jesus call Lazarus from the grave in which he had been lying dead for three days. The stone is rolled back, Jesus tells Lazarus to come out, and lo, there he is, still wrapped in graveclothes. A man who has been dead for days has been miraculously raised from the dead. Did all the witnesses think that? Is it possible to witness such an event and fail to believe that Christ is divine? Failure to believe that Christ is divine is really just a way of rejecting that a miracle has occurred, isn't it? As we suggested above, it seems better to say that one can accept the miracle, not really think there is an alternative explanation of what has happened, and still refuse to accept its significance.

Our question is a serious one because it has to do with the nature of coming-to-believe. Recall what the Fathers of Vatican II said in the "Declaration on Religious Liberty" about Christ's miracles: he worked miracles to shed light on his teaching and to establish its truth. His intention was to rouse faith in those who heard him, and to confirm them in faith, *"not to coerce them."* Consider the following lengthy passage from St. Thomas. It occurs in an article where he asks whether faith is infused in men by God.

"I answer that two things are required for faith. One is that the things to be believed be proposed to man; this is required in order that a man believes something explicitly. The other thing needed for faith is the assent of the believer to what has been proposed. As far as the first of these goes, it is necessary that faith be from God, for those things which are of faith exceed human reason, and would not occur to man if God did not reveal them. To some things are revealed immediately by God, as things were revealed to the apostles and prophets; to others however they are proposed by God's sending preachers of the faith, as is said in Romans 10:15, 'How will they preach if they are not sent?'

"As far as the second requirement goes, namely man's assent to those things which are of faith, there can be a twofold cause. One is an external conducive one, like a miracle seen, or a person's persuasion leading to faith. Neither of these is a sufficient cause: for of those seeing one and the same miracle or hearing the same preaching, some believe and some do not believe.

"That is why it is necessary to posit another interior cause, which moves man inwardly to assent to those things which are of faith. Pelagians say this cause is only man's free will, and that is why they say the beginning of faith is from us, insofar namely as it is from us that we are prepared to assent to the things which are of faith, but the consummation of faith is from God, by whom are proposed to us the things we ought to believe. But this is false. Because when a man, assenting to the things of faith, is elevated above his nature, it is necessary that this occurs in him because of a supernatural principle moving him within, which is God. That is why faith with respect to assent, which is the principal act of faith, is from God inwardly moving through grace" (*Summa Theologiae*, IIaIIae.6.1).

How should we describe the difference between those who believe and those who do not after Christ performed a miracle? Should we say that they agree that they have seen a miracle, but that it is not a sign of the supernatural? Or should we say that they disagree that what they have seen is a miracle?

If we say the last — that the believer says that it was a miracle and the nonbeliever says it was not — we do not mean that the nonbeliever has not witnessed something that startles him and gives him pause. Watching someone cast out devils, or curing illnesses on the spot, walking on water or raising the dead to life, would tend to catch one's attention. At that moment, an opportunity of an enormously important kind is presented to all the witnesses. To accept the grace offered, to believe, is by that very fact to accept what has been seen as a miracle. To refuse to believe when one has witnessed the wonderful deed may take the form of denying that it was a miracle one saw. Whether such a denial makes sense is another question.

The miracle does not coerce belief. But this does not mean that refusal to believe is an innocent option for the witness. The "Declaration on Religious Liberty," having noted that miracles do not coerce or force the assent of faith, goes on to note that Christ denounced the unbelief of those who listened to him. We could multiply scriptural passages in which Christ clearly ascribes moral fault to those who have seen the signs and wonders he has worked and have not believed. To refuse the grace of faith is sinful. Indeed, St. Thomas will argue that the miracles Christ performed *suffice* to show his divinity (*Summa Theologiae*, IIIa.43.4). Does this mean that the miracle is a direct proof of the article of faith that Jesus is both human and divine?

"It is an indirect demonstration drawn from the very certitude of the sign, a demonstration that concludes to the truth of the doctrine because of the absurdities and impossibilities which would follow from the contrary hypothesis. This indirect demonstration does not furnish us, as would a direct demonstration, a clear view of the truth known in itself, but it excludes all fear of error because of the absurdities that error would entail" (*Dictionnaire de théologie catholique*, Miracle, col. 1853). The proof is one of the credibility of the truth proposed, but not a proof of the truth as such.

Must we say that one must already have faith in order to recognize a miracle as a miracle? To see a dead man raised to life is to see something quite outside the ordinary course of events and it would be simply a factual observation that the one doing the raising has powers we would not ordinarily associate with human agents. So far, the miracle does not exceed the realm of ordinary human observations. It is when the implications of this observation make themselves felt that witnesses react differently. What am I to make of this person who raised a dead man to life? As the conclusion that he is himself divine or that he is working with divine power begins to unfold, some witnesses might begin to question the evidence of their senses. So it seems that we can say that initially all the witnesses see is an event that they recognize is quite out of the ordinary, namely, a man commanding a dead person to rise and being obeyed. But if they all thus witness a miracle, they do not all accept the implications of what they have seen, and the refusal to accept those implications may take the form of denying that one saw a miracle.

CHAPTER TWELVE

Between Skepticism and Credulity

When you and I believe in Christ's miracles, we are accepting the veracity of the Gospel accounts. There is no question of personal observation on our part; the miracles are part of revelation which we accept as a matter of faith. So too, when we raise questions like that of the preceding chapter, we are guided by the scriptural accounts, and if Christ blames those who have seen the signs and wonders he worked yet did not accept his doctrine, we will say that the miracles should have sufficed to prove to them that Christ should be believed.

St. Thomas Aquinas distinguished grades of miracles, some being greater than others. If any miracle exceeds the capacity of nature, the more an event exceeds the capacity of nature the greater a miracle it will be.

The greatest miracles are those which exceed nature to such a degree that what happens could never be produced by natural causes. His examples are two bodies being in the same place, or the sun moving east rather than west, or the glorification of the human body.

The second level of miracles exceeds nature, not with respect to what happens, but rather with respect to the subject in which it happens. Examples are the raising of the dead to life and giving sight to the blind. Nature causes life, though not in a dead man; so to see is natural, but not in one born blind.

The lowest level of miracles exceeds the order of nature in the manner of order of happening — as when someone is suddenly cured of a fever by the command of Christ rather than by the customary restorative powers of nature, or when rain falls on command.

Obviously, different things would be said of these different grades of miracles so far as their probative force goes. How does the Church react to present-day miracles?

Consider first of all the cures produced at such places as Lourdes. There are medical facilities at the shrine, and some at least who come in the hope of a cure are monitored during their stay and are subsequently subjected to a good deal of clinical scrutiny if they have been cured. There is no eagerness or haste to pronounce a cure miraculous. Such prudence is not indicative of skepticism. Many miracles have occurred at Lourdes. But accepting that does not entail that one immediately judge that any particular cure is miraculous.

Of course one might undertake the examination of the miraculous in order to show that no miracle is in fact involved. Have not some who studied the Shroud of Turin hoped to show that it could not possibly be two thousand years old? Or to show that the image of Christ was painted on and thus the shroud a hoax? Whatever the hope, examinations have tended to justify the claim that this is indeed the shroud in which Christ was buried. It is said that the image on the shroud, so like a photographic negative, was produced at the moment of resurrection. It would be wrong to say that the Shroud of Turin enables us to *know* that Christ rose from the dead, as if the resurrection were simply the conclusion of a demonstration whose premises were truths about the shroud. But surely such an item, if the reports about it are true, must have a powerfully disturbing effect on the skeptic.

In the process of canonization, it is customary though no longer necessary to find out if any miracles have been wrought by the person whose cause is being pursued. We have seen that sometimes bodies are exhumed and, if they are incorrupt, this is taken to be a sign of sanctity, a divine endorsement of the person. So too the miracles performed. In the chapel of the Carmel of Lisieux where St. Thérèse is buried, there are two stained-glass windows depicting miracles wrought by her and which figured in her canonization; one of them shows St. Thérèse appearing on a World War I battlefield to save a French soldier, while the other shows her appearing in the Belgian Congo to help a missionary priest. Such reports are subjected to close scrutiny before they are accepted.

This kind of procedure is not an exercise in skepticism and obviously it is not an instance of credulity. There are people who have an unhealthy interest in strange phenomena, who hurry off whenever they hear of a new private revelation, who enthusiastically greet any claim that a miracle has occurred, and who consult reports of apparitions as others do astrology charts. A passion for the strange and wonderful as such, forgetting the point of the miraculous, is a serious error. When miracles occur they are meant to turn our minds to God. To see them simply as a source of titillation is a defect.

Conclusion

It is a feature of our minds that we need sensible images in order to form ideas. Consequently, our ideas are, for the most part and in the first place, ideas of sensible things. If we are to come to knowledge of anything other than sensible things, that knowledge must come *through* knowledge of the world around us that we see and hear and feel and smell and taste. Because the world shows forth the glory of God, the world can lead us to awareness of its Maker. "Ever since the creation of the world his invisible nature, namely, his eternal power and deity, has been clearly perceived in the things that have been made . . ." (Romans 1:20).

God gets through to us, not directly — no man has seen God — but indirectly, through his creatures. The remark of St. Paul, quoted above, has long been taken by the Church to mean that human beings can, even apart from revelation, come to knowledge of God from what is evident to them in the world around them. This has been called the charter of natural theology — natural theology being such knowledge of God as humans can achieve in using their natural powers of knowing.

If God indirectly reveals himself in the world he has made, he has also revealed himself in a special twofold way: first, to his chosen people; second, to all men in his Son made incarnate in Jesus Christ. These special revelations, out of the ordinary supernatural revelations, respect the general condition of human knowing mentioned above.

God speaks to his chosen people through the prophets; he appears to the prophets in various sensible ways and makes himself known to the people in the pillar of the cloud, manna in the desert, and so forth. God's presence is first felt in the usual sense of "felt" before a higher spiritual awareness takes place. The happenings, the appearances, the communications which are then written down — all the ways God makes himself known — take into account that men need sensible images if they are to go beyond the sensible. The written words are themselves sensible signs which tell of the sensible manifestations which lead the mind on to God.

That God should take on our human nature, the divine person becoming man, is the most dramatic recognition by God of the demands of the nature he has given us. Christ's incarnation is the act of mercy par excellence: God's lowering himself to our level in order to lift us to his.

Miracles must be seen in terms of the purpose of the incarnation itself.

Sometimes St. Thomas Aquinas speaks of the incarnation as a miracle, but normally by miracles we mean some of the things Jesus did. Could Jesus have gotten through to human beings without performing miracles? The fact that he performed miracles provides fairly good evidence that he judged them necessary if he were to accomplish his mission. Miracles as signs and clues to his divinity provided the setting within which many accepted the grace of faith.

The abundance of the miracles of Jesus, in number and in kind, must strike us. And we find ourselves envying those who were witnesses of them, since our relation to the miracles is by way of the testimony of others. In one of his eucharistic hymns, Aquinas notes that in Jesus the divinity was hidden, but in the Holy Eucharist both the humanity and divinity of Jesus are hidden and both are objects of faith. Our acceptance of miracles, being mediated through revelation, involves a twofold belief.

Of course miracles continue to be performed, and the chief point of them continues to be to call our attention to God, to the mission of Jesus, to those who in a special way have followed him. The miracles of Jesus astounded, frightened, enthralled the witnesses to them, but the point of them was to provide a proof that he was not merely a man among men.

In this book, we have mentioned a number of wonderful things that have occurred during the Christian centuries and particularly things that can be seen today — relics of the true cross, the Shroud of Turin, incorrupt bodies of the saints, apparitions. Taking such things seriously does not suggest an alternative route to the ordinary means of salvation — Mass and the sacraments — since all of the things mentioned above direct us to those ordinary means. Interest in such things merely out of curiosity would be unwise. One's religion might then require a steady diet of such wonders and a loss of the wonder of the Mass and sacraments.

But I suspect that skepticism rather than credulity is the danger today. Too many reserve their wonder for the achievements of technology and regard the world as an arena where man progressively shows his mastery. Such optimism comes hard in this bloody, violence-ridden century. We might even think of that as the message of Mary at Fátima, in Argentina, in Yugoslavia: There is a worm in the apple of the computer age.

It is an old worm. Sometimes it assumes the form of a serpent. We know its eventual fate, but signs and wonders and apparitions remind us of what we must do if that serpent is to be crushed beneath the foot of the Virgin Mother of God.